Candles

Candles

Jon Newman

Thunder Bay
P·R·E·S·S

Published in the United States by
Thunder Bay Press
An imprint of the Advantage Publishers Group
5880 Oberlin Drive, San Diego, CA 92121-4794
www.advantagebooksonline.com

Produced by PRC Publishing Ltd
Kiln House, 210 New Kings Road
London SW6 4NZ

© 2000 PRC Publishing Ltd

All notations of errors or omissions should be addressed to Thunder Bay Press,
editorial department, at the above address. All other correspondence (author inquiries,
permissions and rights) concerning the content of this book should be addressed to
PRC Publishing Ltd, Kiln House, 210 New Kings Road, London SW6 4NZ.

ISBN 1 57145 279 6

Library of Congress Cataloging-in-Publication Data available upon request.

Printed and bound in China

1 2 3 4 5 00 01 02 03

ACKNOWLEDGMENTS

The publisher wishes to thank Price's Candles and the author for supplying all the photography for this book, including the images on the jacket, with the exception of the following:

Pictor International - London for the image on the front cover (bottom middle) and page 84;
The Hulton Getty Picture Collection for pages 7, 11, 13, 15, 16, 61, 62, 63, 65, 66, 68 (top and bottom), 69, 76 (top and bottom), 77, 80 (top), 82 (top and bottom), 85 (bottom), 98-99 (all), 100, 122 and 127;

© Graham Kitching/Swift Imagery for pages 8-9;
© CORBIS for page 27;
© Owen Franken/CORBIS for page 64;
© Paul Almasy/CORBIS for page 79;
© E O Hoppé/CORBIS for page 80 (bottom).

The pictures on pages 20, 22, 23 (both), 31 (bottom), 44-45, 101, 135 (both), 136, 137, 138 (both), 139 (both), 140, 141 (both), 142, 144 (both), 145 (both) and 154 were taken by Tom Wood.

Contents

Introduction

"Be of good comfort, Master Ridley, and play the man. We shall this day light such a candle, by God's Grace, in England as I trust shall never be put out."

Reported as the last words of the Protestant Bishop Hugh Latimer to Bishop Ridley as they were taken to be burnt at the stake in the dry ditch outside the walls of Oxford in October 1555

The world today is full of museums, and these museums are full of forgotten objects, the detritus of the years gone by. We live in an increasingly disposable age where objects become obsolete almost as they leave the shelves. Museum cabinets are brim-full of these once essential but now redundant household goods: the things that no family could live without 200 years ago, 100 years ago, or even 50 years ago. Who now uses wig powder, snuff boxes, sealing wax, and the clothes mangle? Typewriters and carbon paper are turning into historic curiosities before our eyes. Will the same be true of the PC and the fax machine in 20 years time? Where does the process end? And what, in the midst of this self-consciously modern age where nothing endures, are we still doing lighting candles?

Why should such a painfully archaic artifact survive? Its technology is as old and as simple as that of the pan oil lamp used by the ancient Greeks and Romans. Those lamps are now only the concern of the archaeologist and curator. The candle was superceded over a century ago by the revolutionary new technology of the gas light. Yet it is the gas light with its elegant brass fittings and decorative glass shades that now tricks out the antique shop and the reconstructed Victorian heritage center. Electricity killed the gas light. Yet the candle burns on!

Perhaps one of the explanations is the way that the candle has descended to us as a powerful image. It remains as potent to us today as it did to martyred clerics in the 16th century. Macbeth's "brief candle" still reminds us of the fragility of our own existence. The candle is a complex multi-layered symbol that simultan-eously can be made to represent hope, vulnerability, mortality, and determination. The

Above: The candle as a symbol of collective memory; during the Second World War exiled Greeks light candles in the Greek Orthodox Cathedral of Aghia Sophia in London on the anniversary of the Italian Fascist invasion of their country to commemorate their countrymen and women who died.

Overleaf: Christmas candles in the Sagrada Familia cathedral in Barcelona are a reminder of the timeless symbolism of the candle flame.

Introduction

Russian novelist Alexander Solzhenitsyn once described his position as an imprisoned anti-establishment writer in Soviet Russia in the 1960s as being like a candle in the wind. A powerful image that was reprised for the popular imagination by the singer/songwriter Elton John who found it so good that he used it twice: to describe the short tragic lives of both the American film actress Marilyn Monroe and the English Diana, Princess of Wales; both lived their lives "like a candle in the wind."

Steve Biko, the black South African student leader murdered by police in Port Elizabeth in 1977 became an international icon for the evils of apartheid in the 1980s through the words of another English singer/songwriter. Peter Gabriel found in that same image of a candle's flame the words to convey both the loss of a fragile, individual life and the the unstoppable process of change in South Africa that would survive that loss, "You can put out a candle, but you can't put out a fire."

The international charity, Amnesty International which campaigns for human rights and prisoners of conscience around the world uses the logo of a candle burning behind a circle of barbed wire to represent their campaigns against such abuses. The candle-lit vigil, once a very specific part of the medieval Christian ceremonies for the burial of the dead has become secularized and international-ized as a symbol of hope against extraordinary odds. Chinese students at Tianamen Square, Tibetan monks mourning the loss of their nationhood and their spiritual leader, civil rights protesters in the USA in the 1960s have all used candles to make the point of bringing light to the darkness of oppression.

Right: Where there is light there is still hope; Croatian child refugees, trapped in the war in Yugoslavia, suggest both their vulnerability and their optimism through the flames of their candles.

Introduction

1 Candle Makers

"I was at a great loss for candles; so that as soon as ever it was dark, which was generally by seven o'clock, I was obliged to go to bed...The only remedy I had was, that when I had killed a goat, I saved the tallow, and with a little dish of clay, which I baked in the sun, to which I added a wick of some oakum, I made me a lamp; and this gave me light, though not a clear steady light like a candle."

The Life and Strange Surprizing Adventures of Robinson Crusoe, 1719

The finding of a way to make and control artificial light is one of the great unattributable discoveries of the human race. It follows on from the discovery of fire and it predates the invention of the wheel; but beyond that we cannot much say. It is a development that has no date, it does not derive from a single specific culture or location and it is most definitely not the preserve of any individual "inventor." Yet it is one of the defining qualities of human civilization. For humankind to be able to break away from the tyranny of the sun's light and to continue to live and work through the hours of darkness is one of civilization's defining achievements.

We can see just how important an event it must have been to early societies in the way that the discovery of fire has descended to us in myth and legend. In many fire was seen as a magical attribute that humankind could only first obtain by theft. Prometheus who stole it from the gods and gave it to the Greeks and Loki who did the same for the Norse people were both severely punished for their crime. The Phoenicians held that fire was the second major discovery of ancient man, the first one being the discovery of food growing on trees; and light was so important to these people that they were buried with their lamps beside their bodies to show the way through the darkness of the after-life. The Greek historian Herodotus tells of the Egyptian Pharaoh, Mycerinus or Menkaure, son of Cheops, who was warned by an oracle that he had but six years to live.

Right: Bees were kept and harvested from the earliest times. Honey was the initial motive, but subsequently the wax that could be used for candles became just as valuable a product. This engraving shows a hive beneath a fruit tree in the 17th century.

His response was to spend his nights by lamplight feasting and drinking—turning night into day and thus doubling his six years into 12. Artificial light was to be his way of disproving the oracle and cheating death. The fact that he failed in his attempt and apparently died at the end of six years is not the point. The notion of cheating time, of living more fully, of not just seizing but extending the day is a powerful one that works across all cultures and artificial light provided the first practical way of trying to do this.

We can imagine how the discovery of artificial light might have developed. A burning brand pulled from the fire accidentally becomes a torch. The happenstance of meat roasting on a fire led to the observation that animal fat, when heated, liquefies and burns more brightly than other materials. From this it was a small step to identify the fatty portions of an animal, separate them out and use this for illumination. The first containers would have been naturally occurring—a depression in the rock, sea shells, coconut shells, an animal skull. A wick of some sort of vegetable material—twisted grasses, plaited leaves or moss—was a further refinement that controlled the rate at which the flame burnt.

We can state with certainty that stone age man in Europe had arrived at this degree of sophistication 19,000 years ago. The earliest identified use of artificial light is found in some of the caves occupied by Upper Paleolithic tribes in western Europe. The caves at Altamira in northern Spain and of Lascaux in south-west France near Bordeaux have been elaborately decorated with animal paintings. Yet at Lascaux the series of subterranean chambers has always been in total darkness and some of the caves are up to a kilometer from the entrance and daylight. Nevertheless, they contain over 1,500 carefully executed animal drawings. Light would have been essential both to explore the caves and then to carry out and subsequently view the series of animal and hunting scenes drawn on the walls. The artists at Lascaux carved out and used hollows in the rocks to hold

and burn fats with a wick. These primitive fat-burning lamps are the earliest known means of artificial light.

Lamp technology continued to develop and by 3000 BC a number of European and Asian cultures were using quite sophisticated portable lights. Archaeological finds and drawings on tombs and wall paintings reveal a range of saucer-type and wick-channel pan lamps in different materials and designs but all employing the same basic principle. There are ceremonial gold and alabaster lamps from Ur in Sumeria, copper lamps from Egypt, and domestic pottery lamps from Palestine and the Indus Valley. The Mayans in Central America were using similar lamps as depicted on their pyramids. Lamps were in use in China by 2000 BC and pottery lamps in Greece survive from at least 600 BC, although Homer's account of oil lamps at Odysseus's palace—the first written description of artificial light—may be slightly earlier still. These new agricultural civilizations remained fixed in one place and cultivated their lands. They were no longer dependent on following and hunting animals. New crops like the olive tree yielded vegetable oils that could replace animal fat as a light source. Olives were grown all round the Mediterranean and were widely used for lamps. The various Old Testament references to "seven branched candlesticks" in the temples of the Jews are actually a later English mistranslation of the Hebrew word for a lamp. The "candles" of the Bible were really multi-wicked lamps burning olive oil.

The candle was a much later development than the lamp and a considerably more sophisticated portable light source. It was made by repeatedly dipping a long wick in molten fat, that was allowed to cool between each coating, and so building up a thick solid cylinder. Quite how this innovation was come upon is a mystery. It is probably a development from torches made from solid animal fat or resin bound round a fibrous or wooden core. There are depictions of these on Egyptian tombs. The first description of a recognizable candle comes from the Roman writer Pliny. He describes pitch candles with a flax wick and also rush wicks dipped in fat or wax. The candle never supplanted the lamp. In most civilizations it had a parallel existence. But it had several advantages: it was more safely portable; it would not spill its contents; it was less fragile than a pottery container—it would not break or loose its wick; and it was a single unit so that when traveling one did not have to carry separate containers of oil.

From the time of the Romans candles were made from either beeswax or animal fat, known as tallow. This limited range of raw materials remained unchanged until the 18th century. Beeswax was the more expensive; however it was also far superior to tallow. It was harder, it didn't deteriorate, it burnt more brightly yet more slowly, it was odorless, and because it burned at a higher temperature it consumed its own wick and therefore did not require snuffing.

Above: An 18th century French engraving showing the arrangement of straw and wooden hives, types of bee and the beekeeper's tools of the trade.

The Romans knew about their beeswax. Pliny described in detail the different varieties available within the Empire. There was Cretan wax, full of propolis; Corsican wax, where the bees had fed on box tree flowers, was valued for its medicinal properties; Pontine wax, which tended to be full of honey; and Punic or Carthaginian wax from Tunisia, which was the best available. This was a pure white wax that had been bleached in the sun and boiled in brine to refine it. Roman wax served many purposes besides candles—writing tablets, death masks, wax models, and seals. Their wax candle, or cereus, was not primarily a domestic light—oil lamps were used

Candle Makers

in the home. The cereus was a festival light burnt at religious ceremonies; the festivals for Bacchus, Saturn, and Ceres all made use of wax candles.

It was in northern Europe, far from the olive growing regions of the Mediterranean, that the candle developed as the main source of domestic light. Until the middle ages candle making remained predominantly a domestic activity. Wax candles— the preserve of the church and the aristocracy, were made by craftsmen—but the rest of the population made their own tallow candles. A pound of beeswax was a whole day's wages for a laborer, whereas tallow, at a third of the price, was more easily available. Sheep and cattle could be slaughtered all year round, and a good ox might yield up to 80lb of beef fat, whereas the combs of bees could only be harvested once a year and were frequently reserved for the use of the local lord.

The rural domestic economy was necessarily highly self sufficient so all materials for light had to

Above: Victorian beekeepers in their traditional protective costume. The long gown, veil, and hat reduced the risk of stings, while the instrument in the man's hand was used to squirt smoke into the hives and calm the bees so that honey and comb could be safely removed.

be obtainable locally. In the absence of cloth threads, rushes, gathered from local streams and ponds, provided the wicks for homemade dip candles and rushlights. The only difference between the two lights was their dimensions; dip candles were short and fat, rushlights long and thin. Both were made from tallow that was either extracted from the carcasses of slaughtered sheep and cows or—in smaller households which didn't keep their own livestock—collected by the housewife or cook over the year as dripping from roasted and boiled meats. Shakespeare alludes to this process in his famous description of Winter where "Greasy Joan doth keel the pot." Joan is the kitchen maid "keeling" or skimming the fat off the surface of the cooking pot as

Candle Makers

it cooks and storing this to be used for soap and candle making; in the process some of the fat transfers itself to her person—hence her nickname. The Joans of the house normally made the candles too, along with soap. Making it was women's work, generally done in batches through the year in anticipation of the long winter nights. Tallow candles were supposed to improve with keeping and "March" candles made in the spring were reckoned to be the best as they would have a full eight months to improve. A household might not burn any candles through the summer; the long days and short nights meant that people lived by daylight alone. But in winter they would be needed. The poet Thomas Tusser, in his *Advice To Housewives* of 1573 warns,

"Wife make thine own candle,

Spare penny to handle.

Provide for thy tallow, ere frost cometh in

And make thine own candle, ere winter begin."

Rushlights, halfway between a taper and a candle, were the easiest to make in the home. A long rush was peeled to leave the fibrous core; this wick was then dipped once or twice in molten fat and left to cool; mutton fat was reckoned the best material as it dried hardest. Unlike dip candles you didn't have to spend a lot of time building up the thickness with repeated dippings. Suspended at an angle in a simple holder they gave a modest light and a two and a half foot rush burned for one hour. They did not need snuffing, as the wick burned itself up; however they did leave a trail of greasy ash on the floor as they burned. The writer Gilbert White described the picking and preparation of rushes in the Hampshire parish of Selborne:

"As soon as they are cut they must be flung into water and kept there for other wise they will dry and shrink and the peel will not run. At first a person would find it no easy matter to divest a rush of its peel

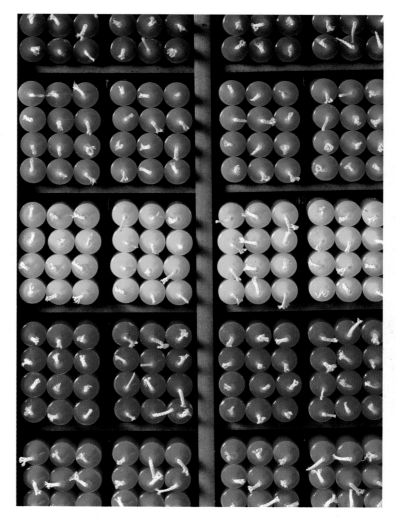

Above: Today this brightly colored selection of candles is unremarkable, but 200 years ago candles only came as white or off white. Only the most special candles, like those for a saints shrine, might be colored or painted.

or rind as to leave one regular, narrow, even rib from top to bottom that may support the pith: but this like other feats soon becomes familiar even to children…When these [rushes] are thus far prepared, they must lie out on the grass to be bleached and take the dew for some nights, and afterwards be dried in the sun.

"Some address is required in dipping these rushes in the scalding fat or grease; but this knack also is to be attained by practice. The careful wife of an industrious Hampshire labourer obtains all her fat for nothing; for she saves the scummings of her bacon pot for this use…

A pound of common grease may be procured for four pence; and about six pounds of grease will dip a pound of rushes; and one pound of rushes may be bought for one shilling."

Above: Today colored paraffin wax candles are the norm, but in the past pure white candles were highly prized—the white was an indication of the finest quality candle that had been obtained by bleaching in the sunlight.

White calculated the cost of this light as five hours for one farthing; but complained that most poor laborers were now wasting their money on purchasing halfpenny candles instead. Samuel Johnson described how in all houses on the remote Hebridean island of Coll "candles are made, both moulded and dipped. Their wicks are small shreds of linen cloth."

There were similarities between the self sufficient existence of Hebridean islanders and that of the settlers of the New World. The puritan colonists of New England took supplies of tallow candles across the Atlantic with them by boat, but they soon ran out. There were no ready supplies of beeswax or tallow for these new communities, but there was plenty of oily fish, which supplied a lamp oil and there was a wild plant, the bayberry, that was found to be useful. The earliest colonists came upon it growing on the sand dunes around Plymouth and Cape Cod. When the fruits were boiled up a wax floated to the surface and was skimmed off and used to make candles. Just as in England, the spring was the normal time for actually making the candles that were then stored over the summer. In 1742 the Reverend Edward Holyoake of Salem, Massachusetts, recorded in his diary:

"On March 23 made 62lb of tallow candles, 29 small and 33.5 great, and on March 22 made 122 bayberry candles, 15lb 12oz."

But by the 18th century the domestic craft of candle making was disappearing fast. Samuel Johnson and Gilbert White, both writing in the 1770s were actually witnessing the last gasps of this tradition. Even then their descriptions were of old fashioned practices in rural backwaters that would have come across as merely quaint to their contemporary London readership who now purchased all their candles from chandler's shops. Candle making had become an urban trade just like any other by the end of the medieval period. Most city dwellers had neither the time or the resources to make their own light. In London the trade had been controlled from the 12th century by the city guilds of wax chandlers and tallow chandlers. These chandlers' guilds were responsible for the pricing and quality of goods and the system of apprenticing to the trade; they also oversaw the standardization of the sizes of candles. In Paris there was an equivalent guild, La Communauté des Chandeliers. Its responsibilities were similar to the London chandlers, but its members also traveled round France, making candles to order at people's houses.

Many London chandlers had their shops and businesses grouped around Candlewick Street in the City, now Cannon Street. These chandlers had a highly developed market and supplied wax round the country as well as for local needs. For instance Canterbury Cathedral was burning over a ton of beeswax candles a year in the 15th century; it was

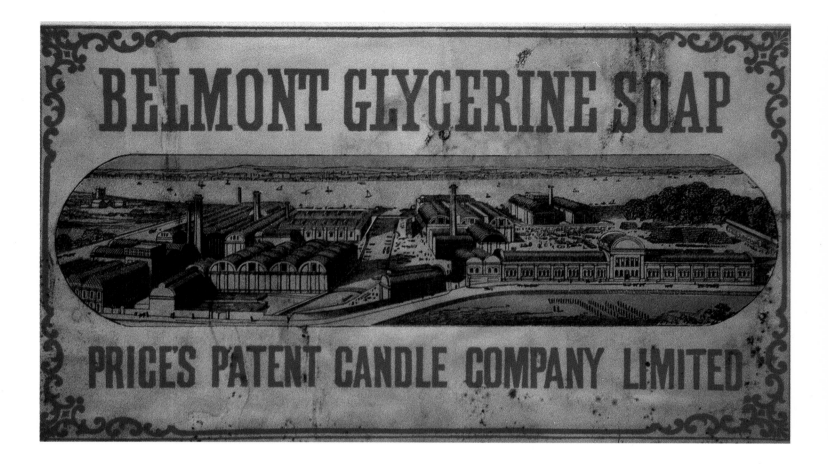

Above and Below: Traditionally soap boilers and tallow chandlers had been overlapping trades; they both used the same raw materials and prepared their tallow in the same way; many candle makers produced soap as a side line and vice-versa.

English encyclopedias of the 18th century. Passages described a process that was still being carried out in workshops by a master and apprentices: a small-scale craft tradition, essentially unchanged for over 1,000 years and that was to continue into the early 19th century. Apart from the introduction of candle molds by the French in the 15th century there had been virtually no technical innovations to candle manufacture since the Roman times.

Tallow chandlers used a mixture of fats from cows and sheep. Beef tallow alone was

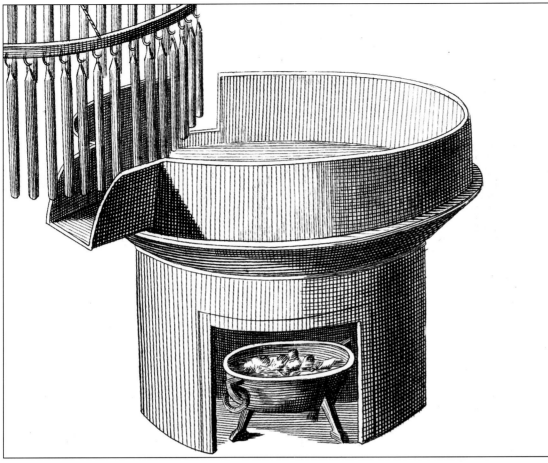

Above: Equipment for pouring beeswax candles in the 18th century. The fire beneath the trough keeps the wax liquid while it is being poured down the candles.

purchased from London wax chandlers, shipped to the port of Faversham by sea and brought on to Canterbury by wagon. Many of these city chandlers were extremely long established businesses: Thomas Field, south of the river on Lambeth Marsh, supplied the wax candles lit to celebrate the birth of the Princess Elizabeth in 1533; and the firm of Fields continued to manufacture candles on the same site up until 1944. The last candle maker in the City of London, Charles Farris, finally left their Bishopsgate works for the suburbs in the 1920s. Even longer established was the Irish candle maker John Rathbone who founded his business in Dublin in 1488 after emigrating from Chester and whose firm continues to trade there today.

The earliest descriptions of candles being made in workshops by chandlers are found in French and too soft and mutton too brittle. Pork fat was out of the question, "making 'em gutter, give an ill smell and a thick black smoak." In France the Parisian Communauté des Chandeliers specified that their members' candles should be of exactly 50 percent mutton and 50 percent beef. The medieval woolen industry in Britain had meant that there was always a plentiful supply of mutton fat. Beef tallow was locally available but had also been imported in quantity from Russia since the 16th century. The chandler obtained these raw materials from local butchers; indeed in the localized economies of market towns their workshops would often be adjacent to the "shambles" or slaughterhouses. The best tallow came from the hard fat or suet located around the kidneys of the animal. It first had to be "rendered" by melting the chopped up suet and filtering it to remove any membrane or other materials. By the 18th century, with the blurring of distinctions between the different trades that the guild system had previously protected, many soap boilers also started to produce candles while tallow chandlers made soap. There was a manufacturing logic to this. Not only were they using the same raw material—tallow—but they were having to render it in the same way.

Once the tallow had been prepared, candles were made in one of two ways—by dipping or by molding. For dip candles the cut lengths of wick were suspended from a rod, known as a broach, or from a rectangular frame, dipped into the tub of rendered

Above: Making poured beeswax candles. The man on the left is rolling a finished candle smooth while it is still slightly soft. The man on the right is building up the thickness of the candles by pouring layers of molten wax down each one.

molten tallow and allowed to cool. Candles were sold by weight and made in different standard sizes reckoned by the number to a pound—"sixes," "eights," "tens," etc. Size was determined by length of wick and by the number of dippings, usually three or four. As demand for candles grew, various techniques were introduced to mechanize the laborious business of suspending heavy frames over a hot tub. A seesaw device with a counterweight and a circular revolving framework from which a number of broaches might be hung were both used. The finished dipped candles were flattened at their base after the final dipping and left to cool before being cut down.

The preparation of the tallow for mold candles was identical to that for dips. The molds themselves were a series of thin metal tubes, generally made of pewter or tin and not unlike a series of cigar cases, recessed into a wooden bench. Wicks were threaded through a hole in the base of each mold and looped and secured at the top by a rod or wire passing through. The molten tallow was poured from a jug into each mold, which was topped up after part cooling and then the bench was removed to the coolest part of the workshop to allow the tallow to harden before the candles were extracted. Mold candles were of a more uniform and attractive

Candle Makers

Above: A tallow chandlers in the 18th century. Typically these were small scale workshops comprising a master and his apprentices. From left to right we can see the tallow being rendered over the fire, wicks being cut at a bench, dip candles being made over a dipping trough, and tallow being poured into candle molds.

appearance than dips and would sell for more. A country parson, writing to a friend in 1795, noted the cost of the locally made dipped candles that the farm laborers in his parish were purchasing compared to his own "Kensington or London Mold candles, 5 shillings for the half dozen pound." He was paying about 35 percent more for the privilege of a pleasing shape.

The whiteness of a candle was seen as an indication of its quality and molded candles might also be bleached to achieve a whiter finish. They were put out in the open air for eight to 10 days at dawn when the candles could be exposed to the both the dew and the rising sun. The results were purely cosmetic; the bleaching made the tallow more closely resemble beeswax and thus allow the chandler to charge more for it, but did not affect the way the candle burned. As a further refinement the most expensive tallow candles were given a final dipping in beeswax. Not only did this give the illusion of a better quality

candle but the harder outer layer of beeswax prevented the molten tallow fat from running down the sides. In the 17th century these were sold as non-drip candles for use in bedrooms.

Wax chandlers prepared their raw material in a similar way to tallow. The beeswax was boiled up and filtered to remove any remaining honey, propolis, or other impurities. At this stage the wax was still naturally yellow. Just as the Romans had valued the bleached white wax from Carthage, so too the church and aristocracy believed white wax candles to be the definition of purity and quality. To achieve this the boiled beeswax was bleached. It was shredded into thin strips and laid outside on tables and over a period of several weeks the wax was repeatedly turned to expose all of it to sunlight. Thus bleached, the white wax was remelted and poured into a large heated tub over which a circular rotating candle frame was positioned. The candle wicks were suspended from this frame and the candles were built up by pouring wax from a ladle down the length of each wick; surplus wax falling back into the tub. The candle was part cooled between each pouring. When the required thickness of wax had built up the candle was rolled between marble or hard wood

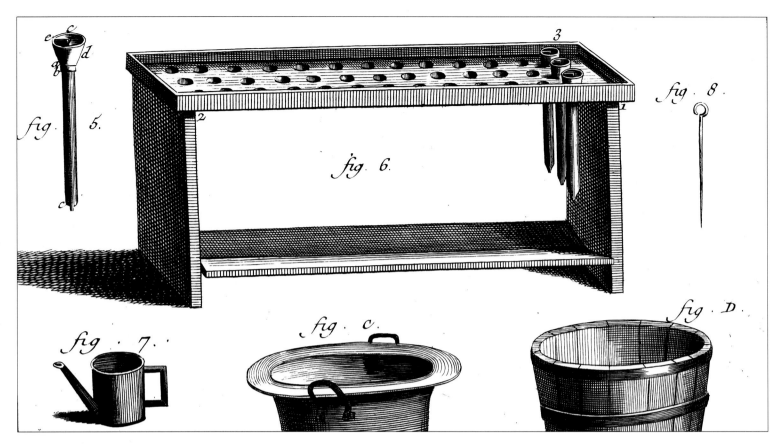

Above: Tallow chandlers equipment: a drilled bench into which the wicked tin or pewter candle molds could be stood, with the various containers for carrying and pouring the tallow.

Right: Tallow chandlers equipment: A broach with tied wicks and a trough for making dip candles and some of the chandlers tools.

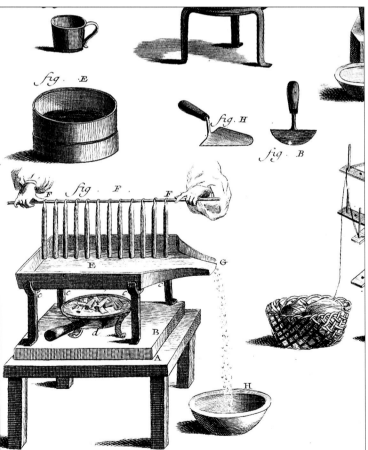

rollers to achieve a symmetrical polished finish. Wax candles could only be satisfactorily made by this labor intensive technique of pouring. They could not be made using metal molds because the wax contracted too much and adhered to the sides. They could be molded using glass molds but these were obviously impractical for large scale production. This combination of a more expensive raw materials and slower manufacturing processes meant that wax candles were between three and five times the price of tallow ones.

If you could afford it the price differential was worth putting up with. Wax candles were the preferred light of the court, the aristocracy, and the wealthy simply because they were a far superior

Above: Beeswax candles for use in church. These are being made by the traditional process of pouring. Although the photograph was taken at Hayes and Finch's candle works in Liverpool in the 1960s, the process has remained unaltered for over five centuries.

product, both aesthetically and technically. They burnt more brightly and more slowly than tallow; they gave off the gentle perfume of bees wax rather than the rancid odor of meat fat; and, because they had a higher temperature flame, wax candles consumed their own wicks. This last factor was extraordinarily important. Tallow not only melted and burned at a lower temperature; it also contained a large amount of non-flammable matter—mainly liquid glycerine—which was the reason the flame was not so bright. A thicker wick was used to counteract the dimness of the flame and increase the light output; but this only created further problems. Because the thick wick was not completely burned up by the lower temperature flame the unburned wick or "snuff" remained within the flame and grew in length as the candle burnt down. If a candle was not snuffed regularly by having the wick trimmed off, two things happened. The light became dimmer and dimmer as the snuff grew in size and the candle would "gutter." Guttering took place when the wick grew so large that it curved over and melted the top side wall of the candle, allowing fat to flow down the candle and form a "winding sheet" of congealed fat on the sides.

The wicks for workshop manufactured tallow candles were originally made from twisted linen rags. However, this linen was in great demand for various other industrial processes. Before the 19th century it was the main raw material for writing paper and competition for the limited amounts of rags was fierce. In 1696 the Scots White Paper Manufactory—the largest Scottish paper maker—actually attempted to get an Act of Parliament to prevent the Edinburgh candle makers from using linen for their wicks. By the 18th century these problems had disappeared. Cheap and plentiful supplies of imported cotton from North America now replaced linen as the main material for wicks, which were now made from three or four thicknesses of spun thread. But the new wicks didn't solve the perennial problem of tallow candles still needing endless snuffing; the problem would not be solved until the development of the "snuffless wick" in 1825. It was discovered that

Above: Candle snuffing is definitely a thing of the past. All candles are now made with a plaited wick that burns brightly without any trimming; a far cry from the tallow candles of previous centuries whose wicks had to be trimmed every half hour.

if the candle's wick could be made to bend into the edge of the flame, which was the hottest part, it would burn itself up and not need to be snuffed. Various versions were produced that would curve over, including wicks that were starched on one side only. The breakthrough was Cambacère's snuffless wick, made from plaited rather than twisted cotton, that naturally turned into the flame. This remarkably simple improvement was universally adopted because it transformed the way a candle burned and the quality of its light. At a stroke it rendered one standard piece of household equipment—the candle snuffer—obsolete. One enthusiastic English parson went so far as to describe the new wick as the greatest invention of the era.

Just as wax candles were more socially desirable than tallow ones, so too the respective occupations of wax and tallow chandler. Wax chandlery was a cleaner and a more respectable trade—and consequently a wealthier one. Tallow chandlery was too closely associated with the slaughtering and butchering of animals: the processes of preparing and rendering the fat for candles on an industrial scale were peculiarly messy and foul smelling. Town dwellers were considerably more robust then and people were prepared to put up with most activities in the interest of wealth creation. So tallow chandlery must have been particularly unpleasant to have been one of very few restricted trades which the authorities could actually prevent from setting up in business—along with other "noisesome and offensive" occupations like night-soil men, horse flayers, soap boilers, and makers of grease for carriages. In both London and Paris all tallow works had been relocated from the city centers by the 19th century.

As populations grew and the world became a smaller place, the pressures to find better or cheaper sources of lighting increased. So too did the expectations of urban society—citizens now required nighttime entertainment at theaters and pleasure gardens, lighting in the home, light in the workplace, and

Above: Atlas Brand candles made in China in the 1920s.

Candle Makers

street lighting. The search was on for new manufacturing techniques and new sources of raw material to light this world. And as exploration and colonialism made the world a smaller place, new possible sources of light were revealed. Native American Indians on the Pacific coast at Vancouver were found to burn a dried oily fish whole for their light. Further North the Inuit lit their igloos with seal blubber lamps. Travelers returned from China and Japan with tales of candles made from insect wax—the secretion of a species of beetle that was collected—and of a vegetable wax made from the fruits of a sumach tree that could also be burnt. In Brazil various species of nuts were used as candles by local tribes; while Jesuit missionaries and explorers in Peru and Venezuela came back with samples of carnauba wax and cow tree gum extracted from trees. In Scandinavia and parts of Germany and Ireland splinters of highly resinous wood—bogwood or fir—were burnt for light. Although called "candlewood" they were really no more than torches. The most intriguing source of light—because seeming barbaric—was found in the Shetland Islands off the North coast of Scotland. The inhabitants used the stormy petrel, a small seabird full of oil, that was trapped locally. A wick was inserted through the dead bird's beak into the oil-rich stomach; the bird was secured upright in a piece of clay and the wick was lit.

But none of these raw materials, fascinating examples of local inventiveness as they might be, could be produced or imported in sufficient quantities to provide an economically viable alternative source of light for urban Europe. The candle makers monopoly on beeswax and tallow remained unchallenged.

It was the North American whaling industry that provided the first serious alternative. European Whalers operating from Nantucket Island at the end of the 17th century, like the Native Americans before them, had first confined their catch to the right whales that came inshore. But there was a larger,

rarer beast out to sea whose flesh, the Native Americans believed, could cure all known illnesses. The first "cachelot" or sperm whale was followed out to sea off Nantucket Island and caught by Christopher Hussey in 1712. In addition to the expected whale oil and flesh in the body, the huge head cavity was found to contain a semi-liquid fat that the whalers called "spermaceti," believing it to be the animal's semen (we now know it to be part of the whale's sophisticated echo-location system). "It looks like a thin kind of candle grease and solidifies almost instantly as it gushes out of the longitudinal cut which the whaler makes at the top of the head."

The quantities obtained—an adult whale contained 10-12,000lb of spermaceti and 60,000lb of sperm oil—justified an industrial scale of processing. The first sperm oil factory opened at New Bedford in 1755, followed by others in Mystic, Martha's Vineyard, and Boston; by the 1840s the U.S. whaling fleet sailing out of New England ports numbered 700 ships. Sperm oil was a superlative lamp oil while the spermaceti, actually a crystalline wax, could be refined and molded as a candle. The light was comparable with that of beeswax—bright and odorless. In 1841 the spermaceti candle became the standard candle for quantifying light output as a number of "candlepower;" ironically this was required to provide a scientific base for calculating the greater luminosity of gaslight. While spermaceti were the candle of choice locally in New England, they were as expensive as beeswax in Europe and remained a minority, albeit high-status, taste.

So there was still an enormous potential market in Europe for a mid-priced candle that gave a brighter, cleaner light than tallow but was not as prohibitively expensive as beeswax or spermaceti. Candle manufacturers finally came up with satisfactory alternatives in the 1830s.

But it was not just a case of "discovering" new raw materials. It was the introduction of new materials in conjunction with the development of scientific

Above: The North American Sperm Whale Fishery found a new use for whale products; in addition to whale oil and whale meat the head cavity of the sperm whale contained large quantities of spermaceti, a crystalline wax that was an excellent material for candles.

processes that was to make the breakthrough. In the 1820s a French chemist, Chevreul, had published his research into fatty acids. He had observed that when a strong alkali was mixed with vegetable or animal fats the solution separated into liquid and solid components. This technique, known as "saponification," was actually the underlying chemistry of soap making, but nobody had previously analyzed what the component parts actually were or considered the implications for candle manufacture. One of the liquids separated out by saponification was "sweet water" or glycerine. This was a non-flammable liquid—and it was the reason tallow candles gave such a poor light. When this glycerine and the other liquid, oleine, were separated off from the alkali/fat mixture what remained was a

hard, pure fat known as stearine. When used as a candle material, stearine gave a brighter light and burned at a higher temperature without the smoke or animal fat smells associated with unrefined tallow. It was also harder and less prone to guttering and dripping.

A newly established London candle maker, Edward Price & Co. quickly saw the possibilities of this industrial chemistry and patented and further refined this stearine process, while simultaneously taking out patents on two newly available raw

Above: Coconut oil extraction in Sri Lanka in the 1830s. The vegetable fat extracted from the coconut was the starting point for Price's Patent Candle Company; it gave them a new inexpensive raw material to make candles from.

materials—coconut oil and palm oil. Price's was now able to refine tallow and vegetable oils to produce "composite" candles—so called because they were now made from a mixture of different fats—which burnt brightly without smoke or smell. The beauty of the chemical process was that it could be applied to any organic fat. A whole range of unsavory raw materials and waste products that had previously been untouchable by candle makers—skin fat, bone fat, fish oil, and industrial waste greases—could now all be rendered into hard white candles. By 1840 the perfect product was ready, just in time for Queen Victoria's wedding. It was traditional for loyal households in England to burn a candle in a front room window on the night of the monarch's wedding. And in London on February 20 most people lit one of

Price's new stearine "composite" candles made from a mixture of refined tallow and coconut oil.

Empowered by industrial chemistry the much expanded Price's Patent Candle Company took on the establishment wax and tallow chandlers. The company invested in 1,000 acres of plantation in Sri Lanka to supply its coconut oil and moved to exploit its second patented tropical product, palm oil. This oil, extracted from the palm nut was harvested and processed in West Africa. Soap makers were already using the oil, but its dark orange-brown color made for unattractive candles. Price's devised a process for cleaning palm oil with sulphuric acid, built themselves a second factory at Liverpool, the port of entry for the West African trade; and a further inexpensive raw material for candles was available.

The improvements for the consumer were dramatic. Good quality light was now almost universally affordable and available. The chemical processes were relatively simple and quickly adopted by other manufacturers to produce stearine wax candles.

PRICE'S DISTILLED PALM CANDLES

There was no need to use tallow ever again. As the writer William Thackeray recalled later in the century, "I think the night-life of society a hundred years since was rather a dark life. There was not one wax candle for ten which we now see in a ladies' drawing room. Horrible guttering tallow smoked and stank in passages. Let us...bless Mr Price and other Luciferous benefactors of mankind for banishing the abominable mutton of our youth."

But it was the wholehearted adoption of new manufacturing technology and production processes in combination with the application of industrial chemistry to unusual raw materials that gave manufacturers like Price's the edge over their competitors. For centuries candle manufacture had remained unchanged. The last major technical innovation—the introduction of pewter candle molds, ostensibly by Sieur de Brez of Paris—had been 500 years ago. But the accelerating culture of innovation and invention brought about by the Industrial Revolution was beginning to impact on candles too. In 1790 Joseph Sampson developed a circular revolving hand frame to speed up the manufacture of mold candles. This was significantly refined by another Londoner, Thomas Binns, in 1801, who added steam heating and water cooling to his revolving frame to make candles

Above: A candle label from 1850 when Price's were using West African palm oil as a raw material for candles. The label shows a candle maker burning through the rope that a slaver has used to tie up an African. In his other hand the candle maker offers the rescued slave the red cap of Liberty. Palm oil was seen as an economic alternative to slavery in West Africa and its use in products like soap and candles was very popular in England where there was widespread opposition to the slave trade.

"more expeditiously and beautifully than heretofore, as there is no necessity for waiting until they are cooled by the air, and when made they will have a better gloss than common candles." In 1834 the first truly mass-production process was patented by Joseph Morgan of Manchester and was in use by Price's at their Vauxhall factory by the 1840s. Candle frames traveled around the factory on a circular railway track and the various processes of continuous wicking, pouring, cooling, and extracting were carried out en route.

The self contained candle molding machine was developed in the USA in the 1840s independently by Willis Humiston and John Stainforth. These free standing machines were a "one stop shop" that carried out all the manufacturing stages in one place. Each machine was capable of producing 50 or 60 candles at a time and used a combination of steam and water to heat and cool the molds. The candles were ejected by

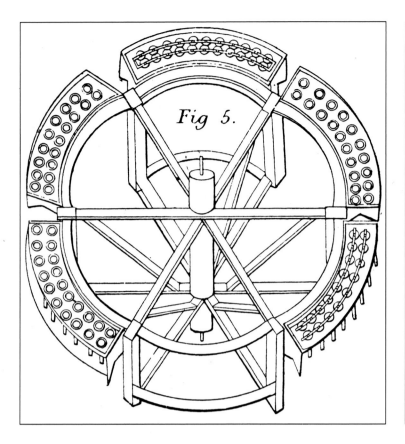

Above: Sampson's candle frame of the 1790s was one of the earliest attempts to speed up the process of candle manufacture. The circular revolving frame contained a series of candle molds that could be filled, cooled, and extracted in turn.

Above Right: Willis Humiston of Troy N.Y. patented his candle molding machine in 1855. It was quickly adopted by candle makers on both sides of the Atlantic. It used a piston to eject the cooled candles and was a significant step in the process of continuous production.

steam powered rams that simultaneously re-wicked the molds for the next set. British manufacturers like Price's had adopted the technology by 1850.

In 50 years the industry had transformed itself from one based around small scale local workshops, manufacturing by hand, and passing on craft traditions from master to apprentice to a full industrial process that used unskilled shift labor in fully mechanized factories. Candle making had previously been a seasonal occupation; the chandlers' workshops closed in the summer when the nights were short and demand was low. In 18th century Dublin, Rathbone's

candle works would shut in June or July and the men would work the harvest on John Rathbone's farm over the summer. By contrast, in 1850 Hawes, a small London candle maker, reduced their workforce from 160 working eight months of the year to just 60 working all year by the introduction of candle making machinery. Big manufacturers like Price's were operating their high-volume plant all year round, 24 hours a day, employing 1,500 workers. The demand for cheap, good quality light that mass production processes could now meet, together with developing export markets, led to a huge capacity for candle production.

However, the opportunity for exploiting the new organic fats like palm oil to make candles was short lived. The discovery of "rock oil" or "petroleum" in Burma in 1854 followed in 1859 by the find of further massive oil deposits at Drake's well in Pennsylvania was to transform candle making as it did so many other industries. The crude oil was processed by the simple fractional distillation process then

Above: Price's Patent Candle Company set up their factory on the River Thames in South London in the 1830s. They were the first candle maker to seriously embrace the principles of mass production; by the 1850s they were employing 2,400 workers in two factories.

Right: A part-mechanized process for candle dipping in use in the 1840s in a Manchester factory.

available and produced four products: benzene, a volatile liquid that was marketed as a leather and furniture cleaner; kerosene, an oil for lamps and stoves; paraffin, a solid wax for candle manufacture; and a heavy lubricating oil. Price's report to its shareholders in 1858 declared "The Paraffine is the most beautiful candle material known, being more transparent than the finest spermaceti."

The candle industry took a little time to adjust to the new product. There were some technical problems with molded candles caused by paraffin's lower melting point, but by 1864 a new method of ejecting the softer candles from molds using compressed air pushed Price's production to 14 tons a day. Paraffin wax carried all before it. In 1870 just 12 percent of candles were made from it; but just 30 years later that figure had climbed to 90 percent. British candle makers now depended on a single raw material and were, for a time, at the mercy of the cartels of Scottish and American oil producers who set the prices. Oil was universally available though; new wells had opened in Indonesia, Russia, Iran, and Mexico by the 1890s. One of the effects of this new dependency on petroleum was to make the industries diversify; Price's now produced lubricating oils and kerosene, while oil companies like Shell and Burmah Oil started making candles.

But by now coming to terms with new materials was actually the least of the candle manufacturers problems. Lamp technology had improved dramatically over the previous 50 years. Before, oil lamps had

FINEST
STEARINE
AND
PARAFFIN
CANDLES

SPECIALLY MADE
FOR
TROPICAL CLIMATES

THE
BURMAH OIL Cº LTD
(SCOTLAND)
MANAGING AGENTS
Finlay Fleming & Cº
Rangoon.

burned no more brightly than a candle and were a far dirtier light source because of their soot. The Argand burner developed in the 1780s used a circular wick and a glass chimney to increase the illuminating power of a lamp ten-fold, while further refinements like gravity feeds, adjustable wicks, clockwork pumps, and flow controls produced a consistent light that needed far less management. The effects were soon felt around the country; by 1812 a Scottish writer was noting,

"The manufacture of candles of excellent quality was formerly carried on in Paisley to considerable extent; and, though the business is still prosecuted, it has also declined. The substituting of oil in place of candles in cotton mills and work shops, and sometimes in private families is supposed to be partly the cause."

If the discovery of petroleum in 1859 had given the candle industry paraffin wax it also provided the burning oil industry with a seemingly limitless supply of cheap kerosene to complement the sperm oil, colza, olive, and other vegetable oils already on offer. Kerosene was lighter than most of these oils and worked well by capillary action, it was almost odorless and smokeless; above all it was cheap. With the development of the twin-wicked Duplex burner in 1865, kerosene oil lamps gave an even brighter illumination and became the light of choice for rural populations in Europe and the United States who still had no access to gas. By 1879 annual U.S. kerosene exports to Europe reached 35 million gallons. Candle makers despaired of "this flood of American petroleum poured in upon us by millions of gallons, and giving light at a fifth of the cost of the cheapest candle."

Even more worrying than these improvements to the traditional oil lamp were the brand new lighting technologies of gas and electricity that were coming on stream by the middle of the 19th century. As early as 1792 a Cornish inventor, William Murdoch, had lit his house with coal gas. By 1822 London's main streets were lit by gas with 122 miles of gas pipes and 40,000 street lamps in place. The cotton mills and factories of Britain's new industrial towns were now operating 24 hours a day. A century before, a laborer might have managed to work 15 hours at a stretch in the summer while daylight allowed, but only half that in mid-winter; the factory hands of the steam-driven and gas-lit temples of industry were now obliged to work 16 hours all year round. By the 1860s gas was starting to become established as the preferred source of domestic lighting, at least for those with the money to pay for it. It was being supplied to the smallest market towns

Above: Candle lit gatherings, like this meeting of the 1877 electoral commission in Washington to discuss the election of the president were soon to become a thing of the past. In 30 years gas and then electricity would quickly make the candle obsolete as the normal means of domestic lighting.

Left: The advent of paraffin wax as the raw material for candles meant that traditional candle makers were now competing directly with the new oil companies who could also make candles as an inexpensive sideline to their main business. This Burmah Oil label dates from the turn of the century.

Right: Stearine candles described products that could have a number of ingredients.

in England and new town houses for the middle classes were now being built with pipework for lighting ready installed.

Two new developments by 1895 assured the continued dominance of gas in the domestic lighting market. The introduction of the penny coin slot gas meter finally enabled the working classes to afford to pay for gas on a daily basis and abandon their candles and lamps. But it was still an expensive form of light, as one London child of the turn of the century later recollected. "Gas burned up the pennies. So to save the gas we used a candle in the bedroom. The hallway and toilet had no light, so we put a paraffin lamp on the wall." The second critical development was the "incandescent" gas mantel, which gave a significantly brighter light and, as well as putting candles further in the shade, allowed gaslight to compete with the newer electric lighting that was becoming available. Gas lighting remained attractive to the poor into the 20th century because it also doubled up as a source of heating. By 1903 the inverted gas burner enabled gas "to cast a downward light free from shadows," while pneumatic gas switches allowed gaslights to be switched on instantaneously, just like electricity.

Wax Overflow on Tank
Behind Angle

Clamps

Candle Holder
Wooden
Battens

Tank

Piston
Rods
Adjusting Nuts

Wicks

Water
Over-
flow

Rack, &
Pinion

Lever

Spool Box

Photo. 'A.

See R.S.P.Cº's Letter dated 7.10.26

No. 2058

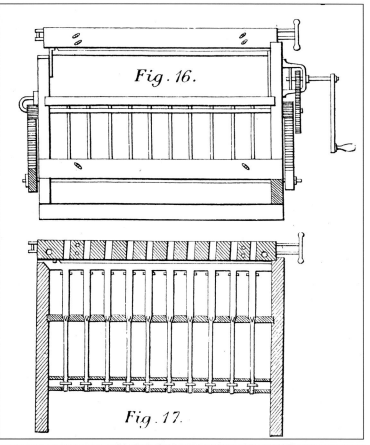

Fig. 16.

Fig. 17.

By 1890 the wealthy were about to be seduced by an even newer technology, electric light. Humphrey Davey had demonstrated his new electric arc lamp to the Royal Society back in 1808. This prototype worked by a high voltage current bridging an air-gap between two carbon poles. The illumination was intense—1,500 candlepower could be achieved—but the carbon rods would burn up in under an hour. It required a further 70 years development, culminating in the simult-aneous invention of the vacuum filament light bulb by Joseph Swan in England and Thomas Edison in the U.S.A. in the late 1870s, before a practical form of domestic electric light was available. The stark blue light of the arc light was occasionally used for ballrooms and public lighting at an earlier date, but never in the home. London's first public electric supply system was operating at Holborn Viaduct by 1882, the same year as the Pearl Street power station in New York. Before then electric light was only available to the complete enthusiast prepared to generate his own electricity—like the Scottish businessman W.G. Armstrong whose electric lit house—the first in the U.K.—used a water turbine as a generator. Once electricity became generally available, the effects were dramatic. It is estimated that in the U.S. the average household increased its domestic lighting 20-fold between 1855 and 1895. In England the adventurous and those who could afford it were having the gas pipework ripped out of their town houses to be replaced by electric "flex." The vacuum light bulb, equivalent to 100 candles, that brought "a crude white glare into every crack and cranny of life," was so bright that people using it actu-

Far Left: A steam heated and water cooled, self wicking candle machine as used in the 1920s in Japan.

Above Left: John Stainthorpe of Buffalo N.Y. patented his candle machine in 1855 just months before his rival Willis Humiston. Humiston and Stainthorpes' basic design informed candle molding machinery for the next century.

Left: Ordinary white household candles were about to become a thing of the past as more and more households turned to gas or electric light.

"Art" candles from Price's catalog of 1909. Elegant shapes, color, hand painted designs, and even perfume helped transform the utilitarian household candle into a new luxury product.

Candle Makers

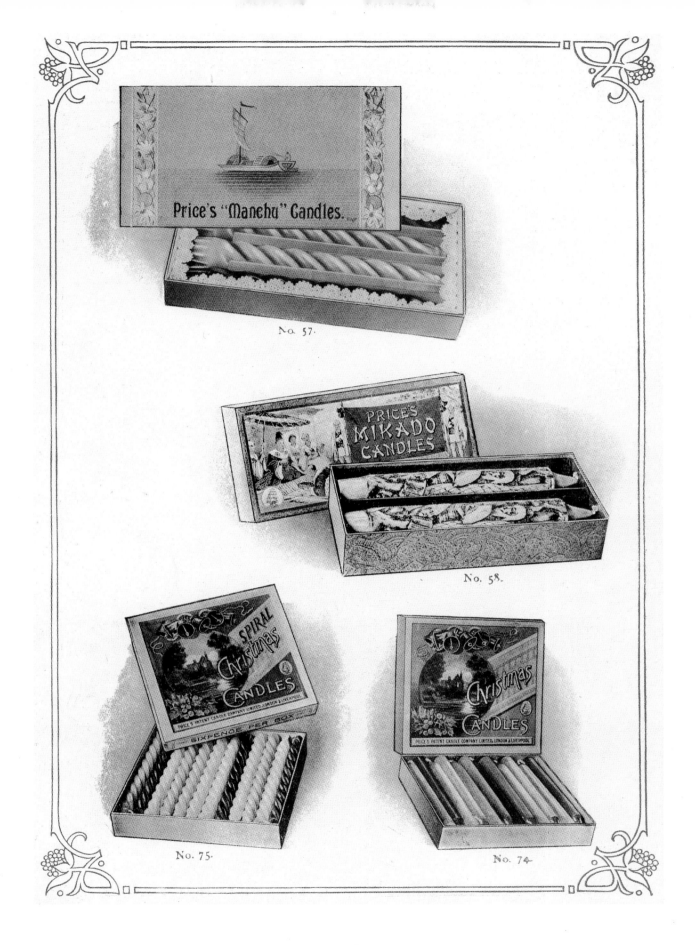

No. 57.

No. 58.

No. 75.

No. 74.

Candle Makers

FINEST
MINERAL
WAX
CANDLES

SPECIALLY
MADE FOR
TROPICAL CLIMATES.

THE
BURMAH OIL CO LTD
(SCOTLAND)
RANGOON

Managing Agents
FINLAY FLEMING & CO

ally had to have a "light shade" to protect their eyes. Candles were about to become the last resort of the underclass.

Candle manufacturers had to react to these pressures. Burning oils, gas, and electricity between them forced the price of candles lower and lower. The percentage profit on units of manufacture shrank and candle makers could only remain in business by increasing the volume of their output and reducing their production costs. There was continued heavy investment in new machinery through the 1880s to create even more efficient molding machines and continuous production processes. New foreign markets were opening up in Australia and the colonies, as yet untouched by gas and electricity and still in need of candles. But in an increasingly international marketplace there was sharp competition with Russian, French, and Dutch candle makers. In a business with increasingly tight margins small companies went to the wall. Price's, now the largest U.K. candle maker, took over eight other London manufacturers in the 20 years between 1892 and 1912. Oil companies like Shell and soap makers like Levers gobbled up the rest.

But there was a limit to what could be achieved by technical and manufacturing efficiencies. The unit cost of a candle could not be continuously reduced; and anyway the underlying problem was that the mass domestic market for candles as the principal source of light was shrinking dramatically. Candles were no longer one the basic requirements of life they had once been; instead they were becoming the emergency light of last resort when the electrics fused or the gas ran out. If the business was to survive at all, then manufacturers had to reinvent the candle. It was pointless for candles to compete directly with the new types of light. Instead they would be presented as beautiful or elegant sources of additional light that could continue to be used in spite of and alongside these newer forms.

Back in 1850 the quality of a candle was still solely determined by "technical" considerations: the amount of light it gave, whether it smoked, smelt, dripped grease, or needed snuffing. They were still sold by weight; and the sizes—eights, tens, twelves, etc.—denoted the number to the pound and merely determined the burning time. Even a major manufacturer like Price's was only producing 18 different shapes or sizes of candle; smaller makers offered far less choice. But if the innovations of the first half of the 19th century had been about raw materials and chemical and industrial processes, then those of the final decades of Queen Victoria's reign were to do with the aesthetics of the candle. Candle makers discovered designers and designers introduced new shapes, the use of color, and new ways of marketing and packaging candles.

Colored candles were a real novelty. Previously the makers' preoccupation had been with the whiteness of the candle—time and money was spent bleaching beeswax and tallow to achieve it. The wealthy had occasional access to colored wax candles, dyed with red lead or vermilion, but for the rest of the population candles came in white, white or, more cheaply, off-white. One of the reasons that stearine had been so successful in the 1840s was because its hardness and whiteness so closely resembled that of expensive beeswax. Conversely, palm oil candles had only become acceptable after a way was found to remove the strong color; the first dark orange palmitine candles had not been a success. With the advent of paraffin wax all household candles were a uniform white and increasingly unremarkable in the gas-lit, highly ornamented households of late Victorian Britain and America. The chemistry of aniline dyes came to the rescue and made bright colors easily available so that by the 1890s color became an important selling point—Venetian red, Indian yellow, and Eau de Nil candles breathed new life into old products. Victorian inventions like Christmas and birthday cakes created their own special requirements: gold, red, and green candles suitable for attaching to Yule logs, Christmas trees, and cakes.

Left, Above, and Right: As the domestic market for candles shrank in the face of competition with gas and electricity, candle manufacturers moved to exploit developing world markets where candles were still a necessity or where, in the case of Price's new factories in Latin America, like the one at Portales in Chile above, the huge amounts of candles burnt by Catholic church-goers guaranteed sales.

Right: Price's opened factories in China, Chile, South Africa, Thailand, India, Sri Lanka, and Zimbabwe where they produced candles to meet the local cultural needs of the host country as this trade stand at Nankin, China in 1912 shows.

❊ 44 ❊

Candle Makers

Left: Pugin's Medieval Chamber at the 1851 Great Exhibition in London was a defining moment in the Victorian development of Gothic taste. The tapered candles and medieval candlesticks and pricketts displayed there were to influence domestic taste for the next half century and encourage new shapes and designs for candles.

Candle Makers

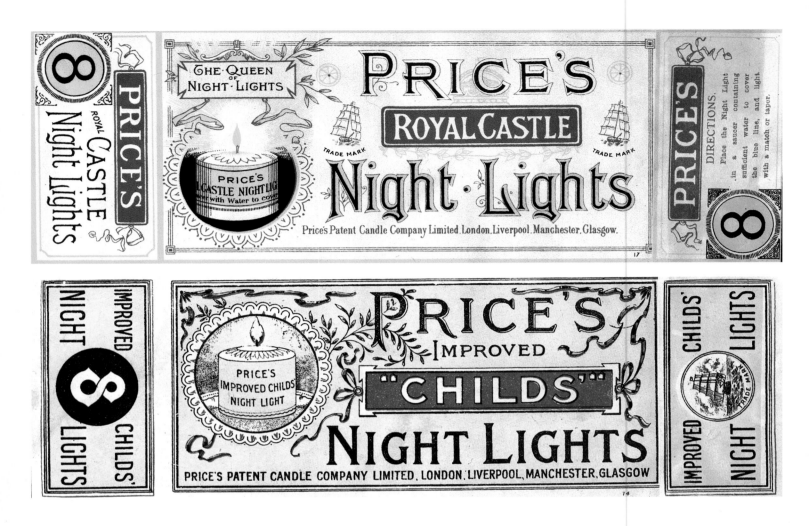

Above: Night lights were widely used to light rooms, especially children's bedrooms and to warm food. These labels date from the 1890s.

One other important area of innovation was in the shape of the candle. The cost benefits obtained from the use of candle molding machinery and mass production processes had also imposed a cylindrical uniformity on the product; every candle looked the same shape. This might initially have appeared "modern" to the early Victorian eye in comparison with the variations in the handmade candles of an earlier age, but by the end of the Victorian period this hum-drum sameness was losing its appeal. The Pre-Raphaelite art movement, William Morris's return to a craft tradition, and the growing Victorian taste for things Gothic all in their different ways influenced the basic design of candles. Elegant new shapes like the

tall tapered Venetian candles echoed the new medievalism of Gothic designers like Pugin, while further developments to candle making machinery such as "rifled" molding machines allowed for the mass production of intricate new candle shapes. Spirals, flutes, cables, and candles with self fitting ends started to replace the utilitarian shapes of the mid-century. Price's were making 130 different named and specified candle sizes by 1900.

Another approach was the deliberate diversification and packaging of different candle products. Where a previous generation would simply have purchased their candle by size, now a whole range of specific candle types was suddenly available. The dining room, the ball room, the bed chamber, and the servant's room all had their own named and specified candle—those for the servants' bedrooms only lasted for 30 minutes. Candles started to be re-packaged for

Candle Makers

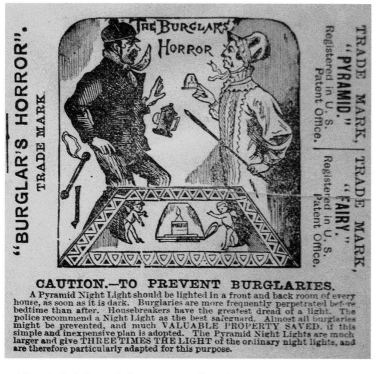

Above: Clarke's Burglar's Horror. Candle makers were increasingly on the lookout for new ways of selling old products. The candle as crime prevention was one such; customers were urged to light a "Burglars Horror" in the window of every downstairs room to guarantee a crime-free night.

Right: Shade candles, designed to burn beneath ornamental lampshades were one way that the candle industry attempted to compete with the newer attractions of gas and electric light. Even if the light wasn't as bright, the user could at least indulge their taste for ornamental lampshades.

every conceivable use: carriage candles designed to burn in spring loaded glass carriage lamps and bicycle lamps, piano candles to burn in sconces either side of the music stand, photographic darkroom candles, and even the "Burglar's Horror" night light (to be lit in every front and back window and guaranteed to scare off criminals). By the 1890s makers were producing opaque, hard white candles that could burn beneath a lamp shade without smoking, enabling the candle user to participate in the fashion for decorated lampshades so popular with gas and electric lighting. Samuel Clarke, a London and U.S. manufacturer introduced the "Fairy Light" range of decorated glass containers designed to burn night lights. They even, perhaps

PRICE'S

GOLD MEDAL PALMITINE SHADE CANDLES

SELF FITTING

PRICE'S PATENT CANDLE COMPANY LIMITED · LONDON AND LIVERPOOL

PRICE'S GOLD MEDAL

SS 12 SELF FITTING

PALMITINE

WINDSOR CASTLE

TRADE MARK

PRICE'S PATENT CANDLE COMPANY LIMITED, LOND

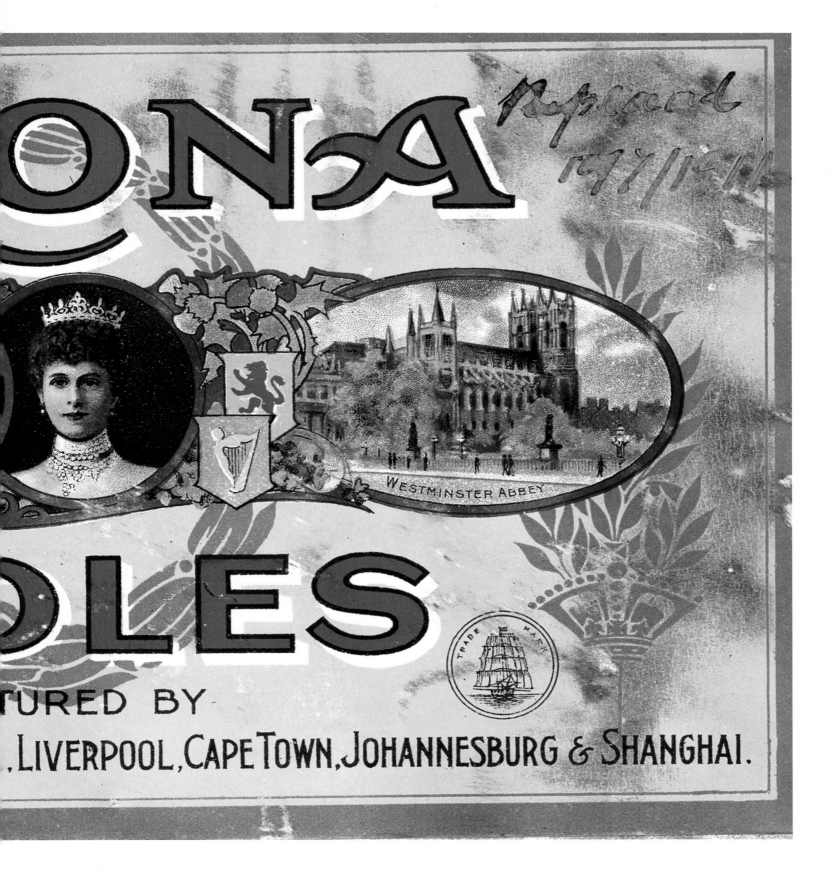

WESTMINSTER ABBEY

TRADE MARK

, LIVERPOOL, CAPE TOWN, JOHANNESBURG & SHANGHAI.

Above: An almost guaranteed way of selling products to the loyal citizenry of England before the First World War was by making reference to the royal family. Price's produced this label for its premium Corona candles to celebrate the coronation of King George V and Queen Mary in 1910.

Candle Makers

Left: Price's produced special long-burning candles for the emigration ships sailing to North America and Australia in the 19th century. The fire risk from candles in overcrowded passenger areas below decks was so great that they also manufactured a lockable safety lantern to be used with the candles.

Top Right: Piano candles were one of the "niche" markets that developed in the 1890s; along with dinner table candles they were seen as one of the more sophisticated ways in which candles could continue to be used.

Left: This advertising for Clarke's Burglar's Horror night lights in the 1930s compares the theft of treasures from Cheop's pyramid with the greater security obtained by the users of the night light.

Above: Mining candles were made of harder stearine. This stopped them melting in the hot environment at the bottom of a mine; it also meant that in extremis they were edible. Many miners survived disasters underground by eating their tallow or stearine candles.

Right: Clarke's Double Wick candles for the dinner table. Candle light was to remain a fashionable and sophisticated way of illuminating the dining room long after other rooms succumbed to gas and electricity.

optimistically, produced a conversion kit that allowed you to turn a gasolier into a chandelier by replacing each gas burner with three Fairy Light holders.

Harder tallow stearine candles were marketed for coal miners, navvies, engineers, emigration ships, and use in the tropics. Such candles were also edible—as trapped miners and stranded lighthouse keepers had overed in the past—and a minor niche market developed in the early 20th century supplying explorers like Scott, Mawson, and Shackleton with candles that could, in extremis, be eaten. Today, the British Army includes edible "Table Lamp No. Two" stearine candles in soldiers' emergency rations for the same reason.

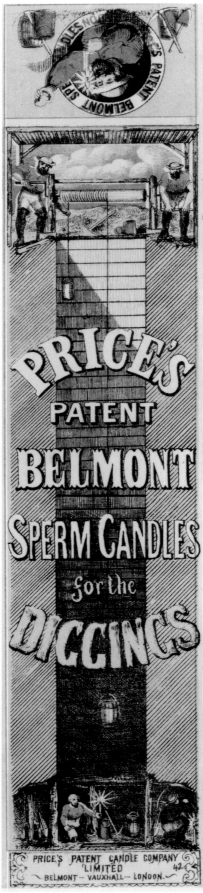

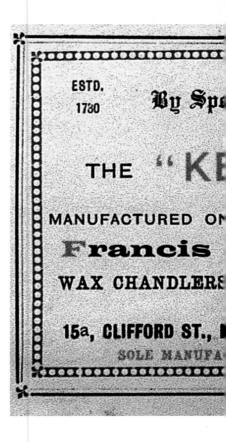

Left: Candles for miners, navvies, and engineers. In the 19th century the terms for raw materials were used deliberately vaguely—sperm, tallow, palm, wax, and stearic acid could all be used to describe a stearine candle as here.

Above: Tucker's were an established London firm from the 18th century, originally based in Kensington. After 1906 they developed a specialist niche market supplying the Roman Catholic church with "percentage" beeswax candles for the high altar.

Below: This stylish label for a hand painted 1890s "art" candle uses French terms and motifs to suggest elegance and sophistication.

Candle Makers

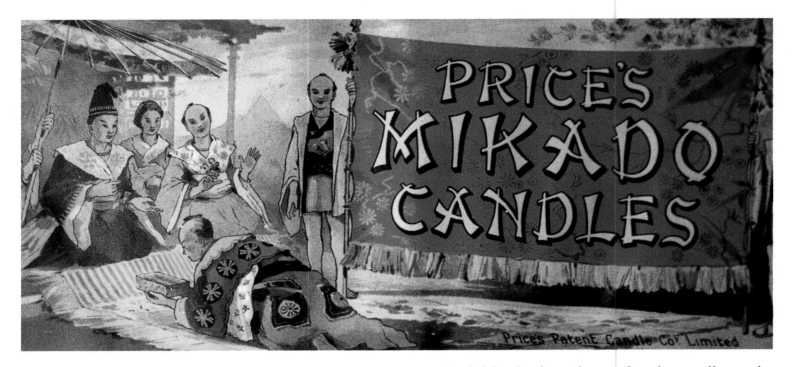

Above: Gilbert and Sullivan's 1885 operetta, "The Mikado," introduced a fashion for things Japanese. This candle label from the 1890s was one of Price's more successful decorated candles.

One user of candles whose requirements for large quantities did not change was the church. While most candle markets were in decline, the growth of the High Church movement in England in the second half of the 19th century with its return to Catholic inspired ritual and the extensive use of candles actually saw the church market increase. The London candle makers, Frances Tucker and Charles Farris, both long established general candle makers, reinvented themselves as church candle makers, respectively catering for the Anglican and Catholic church. The Liverpool firm Hayes and Finch started up in 1880 as a specialist Catholic church candle maker. In 1906 Tucker's and Hayes and Finch obtained the agreement of the Catholic bishops of England and Wales that all candles burned at Mass should contain 65 percent beeswax, thus guaranteeing a market for their beeswax "percentage candles." The percentages may have fallen, but both Anglican and Catholic churches today still require high altar candles to contain a proportion of beeswax and Hayes and Finch are still the main U.K. supplier.

Probably the best future for the candle at the beginning of the 20th century lay in its reinvention as an art object. The introduction of new shapes and colors was successful in creating new demands for candles as ornamental objects. The logical extension of this was the creation of the "art" candle; an object that would be so exquisitely designed and ornamented as to beg the question whether its owner would ever want to light it. Art candles reversed the whole trend of candle manufacture over the previous century, which had been a constant striving toward automation, and low-cost mass production. Designs like the "Mikado" and "Chinese Dragon" candles that Price's introduced in the 1890s combined state of the art three dimensional molding with labor-intensive hand painting and finishing to produce exquisitely finished and packaged objects whose principle purpose was no longer to give light but to provide decoration. These were followed by designs like the blue and white painted "Willow Pattern" candles and the "Jazz" candle of 1924 as well as various Art-Deco inspired styles like the "Venetian" in the 1930s that combined candles and co-ordinated candlesticks as a designed set. The logical extension of the argument that the candle was primarily a decorative object

A PRICE'S MATCHED CANDLE SET

VENETIAN

SET No. 8

was for the candle manufacturer to produce both the candle and its holder.

Even though the market for standard household candles was shrinking, it was still big enough to justify further developments in manufacturing processes. The cold extrusion process was a highly automated process developed in Germany in the 1940s to further reduce production costs. As the name suggests it dispensed with heat and molten wax and instead used pressure to convert crushed or powdered paraffin wax to shape. The wax was forced through a small orifice on an extrusion machine, where it consolidated round a wick, producing a continuous length of candle, that would be mechanically cut to length. The process was not unlike like squeezing toothpaste out of a tube. Extrusion could initially only be used for small-diameter, parallel-sided candles and became the staple method for making household candles.

Candle making continued to change dramatically through the 20th century. As late as 1914 more than half the population of the U.K. used neither gas nor electricity and therefore must have still been burning candles or oil lamps for light. But by the end of the 1950s electric light had completely replaced oil, gas, and candles as the domestic light. Candle consumption was only 7,000 tons in 1960; that was less than a sixth of what had been used annually during the First World War. Candle makers' automated processes allowed them to reduce the costs of the candles they manufactured. But technology alone was not going to solve the fundamental problem of how you got people to continue to purchase a product that was now completely obsolete.

Left: As the Art Deco style became more popular in the 1930s it influenced design in all sorts of areas including candles and candlesticks.

Above: 1930s export label for the British colonies.

Candle Makers

Candle Makers

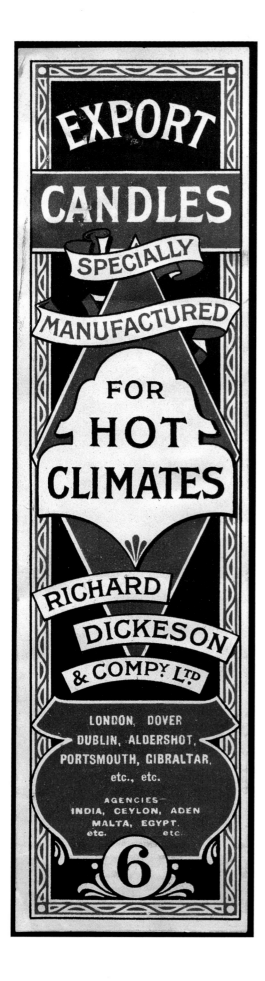

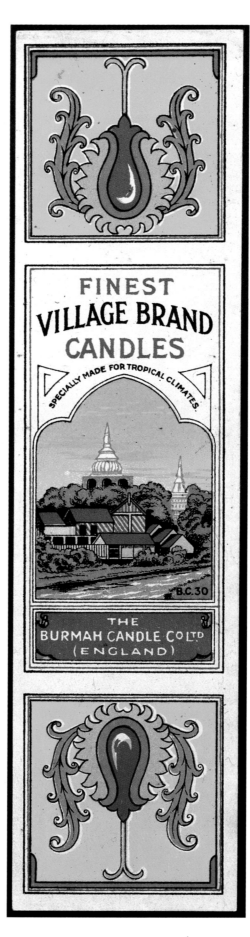

Left: Export candles for the tropics tended to be made of harder stearine instead of paraffin as they were less likely to lose their shape.

Right: Candles produced for the year of Queen Victoria's Diamond jubilee in 1897.

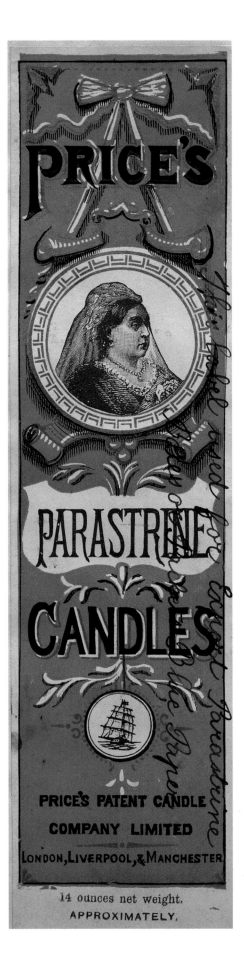

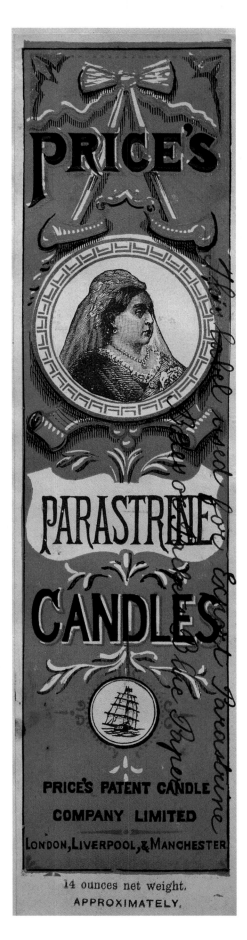

Candle Makers

2 Candle Users

Sacred Light

At an early stage in most societies a division developed between two sorts of light: sacred and profane. There was one light that people merely used to see and live by, and another light that came to represent the god or deity that was a sacred light under the control of priests. The sun had been worshipped by almost all early societies and it was a simple translation of ideas to use fire, lamps, or candles to represent that divinity. The worshippers of Zoroaster, in Iran, honored their sun god by burning candles. When Islamic persecution drove them to India in the eighth century they carefully took their sacred fire with them and relit it in their new home. Many other faiths have or had their candlelit or lamp lit mysteries: candles were used in Attica in Greece for the Eleusinian mysteries in honor of Ceres; fires were used by the Aztecs to honor their gods; and candles are still burned in Sri Lanka before images of the Buddha. In Fes in Morocco, Muslim celebrations for the prophet Mohammed's birthday involve the burning of 30 pounds of candles throughout the day and night. The Roman festivals of Bacchus, Saturn, and Ceres all made use of wax tapers.

In Judaism, too, God was conveniently represented by the flame of an oil lamp, and the miraculous survival of the holiest of holy flames, the lamp that burned in the temple of Jerusalem, is celebrated annually at the feast of Chanukah. Here the "haukkiyha," the eight-wicked lamp or eight-branched candlestick recalls the temple light that kept burning during the desecration of Jerusalem in 165 BC. One flame is lit on each day to represent each of the eight days that the temple lamp continued to burn unattended before the city was relieved by Judas Maccabeus. For Orthodox Jews the candle remains an important part of their personal Sabbath celebrations as well. Two candles are lit before the meal on Friday night to remember and sanctify the Sabbath and another candle is lit on Saturday night in a special Havdalah candlestick to signify the close of the ceremony. These candlesticks have a very high significance. Like the sacred flame of the Zoroastrians they provided a continuity for a displaced people and are treasured family relics.

How was one to distinguish between a candle flame that was holy and one that was functional? In Christian churches today it is obvious. The only candles burning are those on the altar; the rest of the church is probably lit by electricity. But 100, 200, or 500 years ago that distinction did not apply. Instead it was the different type of candles burned that defined their purpose. Ordinary tallow candles burned in the body of the church, while pure white

Right: An early astronomer in Holland works at his star charts by candle light. The candle flame lit the way forward for scholars and scientists as well as harking back to religious superstitions of an earlier age.

Above: The crowning of the Queen of Light at the celebration of St. Lucy's day on December 13 at a Swedish church. This Christian ceremony is an example of the use of candles to perpetuate a pre-Christian winter lights festival: in this case the Viking ceremony of Jol or Yule.

candles made from beeswax were reserved for the altar. The same distinction was applied in Judaism where the eight-branched lamp or candlestick used for Chanukah had eight lights to be lit for sacred reasons, but also had a ninth "servitor" light attached— a lamp or candle that was not sacred but instead provided the light to see what you were doing.

The Romans reserved the use of beeswax tapers, or "cereus," for their religious ceremonies while they lit their homes with oil lamps. Perhaps it

was from this religious use of the cereus that the early Christian Church developed its own use of beeswax candles. Candles were first used for secret worship by the early Christian communities in the catacombs at Rome while the earlier worship of Roman gods continued to be practiced. Bees and their wax already had mystical associations in many cultures and religions. The Egyptians believed the first bee to have been created from a teardrop of the god Ra and the Mayans worshipped a bee god named Al Mucan Cab. Bees were regarded as sacred by the Bronze Age forest dwellers of Europe. The land of milk and honey is not even exclusive to the Jews; honey features in the afterlife of Muslims, Vikings, and Celts as well.

Candle Users

The early church adopted the beeswax candle for its rites and by the Middle Ages had made all sorts of elaborate theological justifications for its use in worship. Bees were believed to come from Paradise. They died in the process of making wax and honey and this sacrifice was compared to Christ's death on the cross. The medieval theologian Ennodius of Pavia likened a candle to the Trinity where the rush wick was the product of water, wax was the offspring of virgin bees, and the flame was sent from heaven. This was all retrospective justification after the event. Undoubtedly one of the reasons beeswax candles were burned on the altar while dirtier, dimmer tallow candles were used in the body of the church was simply because they were the best available and the quality of this light made it more appropriate for the spiritual freight it had to bear. Light had an important symbolic value for the church. In the conversion of the pagan races of Europe, the candle provided the perfect portable symbol; light, quite literally, was being brought into the darkness.

It was the church, and specifically the monasteries and religious houses, that first used the power of artificial light to be able to ignore the distinction between day and night. The rest of medieval society lived by the sun, rising with the dawn and returning to bed at dusk; days were short in winter and long in summer, but whatever the time of year you went to bed with the sun. Monks and nuns were the glorious exception to this, the first practitioners of a 24 hour lifestyle, their lives were given over to a continuous cycle of worship and prayer at set hours of both day and night. The offices of compline, lauds, and matins were performed through the night. In addition to the candles used for mass, this daily recital of the canonical hours meant that artificial light was essential. All religious houses had a sacrist or ferertrans who had specific responsibility

Right: Giant and elaborately decorated candles made in Cuzco, Peru, are a conflation of Christian and pre-Christian Inca symbols.

Candle Users

Above: An altar boy bears a ceremonial candle for the Christmas mass at a church in Kaysersberg, France.

was lit on Easter Saturday and not put out till Ascension Day, 40 days later. Although churches would normally buy in their wax from a chandler, the candles might still be made up in the church behind the altar or in the rood loft. The candles were often produced in a batch for Candlemas on February 2; the feast that celebrated the purification of the Virgin Mary and the admission of the infant Christ into the temple. It was so named because the congregation would process to the church with lit candles and at this service the priest would bless all the altar candles for the coming year.

The other church service that made especial use of candles was Tenebrae—Latin for darkness or shadows—at the end of Holy Week. This was one of the most dramatic services in the calendar with an almost theatrical use of light. Fifteen unbleached wax candles were extinguished one by one during the course of the service to represent the desertion of Christ by his disciples and followers; the service ended with the church in complete darkness representing the "tenebrae" of the crucifixion. The symbolic power of candles was also an important part of the feast of St. Blaise. Blaise was a fourth century Armenian Bishop, with a reputation for curing diseases of the throat. His feast day is February 3, the day after Candlemas, when traditionally cures were performed by the laying of the crossed candles on the throat of the supplicant.

for making the huge quantities of wax and tallow candles required.

Ordinary churches in the Middle Ages might not require quite as much lighting as a monastery, but their use of candles was still high. A large cathedral like Canterbury could burn over 2,000 pounds of wax a year while even a small parish church got through about 100 pounds of beeswax. Most of this went on the "beam light" that remained constantly burning on the candle beam above the rood screen. Other requirements were for the altar candles, font lights, and the paschal candle—a giant candle that

In the Middle Ages a huge cult developed around the relics of Christian saints enshrined in cathedral churches. Pilgrims criss-crossed Europe on devotional journeys to say prayers and make offerings at these shrines. The English shrines of Thomas of Canterbury, Our Lady of Walsingham, Richard of Chichester, and Edward of Westminster were all popular destinations. A saint's relic was an enormously significant addition to a church, both in terms of status and the income that might derive from it and no expense was spared in presenting them. The brilliant illumination of the shrines was dramatic and eye catching; they were delibarate focal points in otherwise gloomy buildings, "placed on high as on a candlestick to enlighten the church." Wax lights surrounded the shrines and burned all through the day and night; in some cases these candles were painted or elaborately decorated. St. Thomas' at Canterbury famously had eight candles on the shrine and another four on the altar "which ought to be decently painted in red and green, one red and the other of a green color with roses and

Above: The lying-in-state of King Edward VII at Buckingham Palace, 1910.

flowers of gold and other colors subtly inserted." The shrine of the three kings of Cologne in Germany was similarly and opulently adorned with painted candles.

As well as being an essential element in the theater and spectacle of the church, candles were also important as offerings or votive gifts. Pilgrims always made a votive offering at the shrine. This was traditionally a beeswax candle, and was a useful source of income to the cathedral who sold the candles to the pilgrims. Many pilgrimages were made to cure an illness, so to make the votive gift more effective it often represented what the pilgrim was seeking. Sometimes the beeswax was modeled to the shape of the afflicted area—a broken limb or a sore head—or "measured candles," the height or weight of the person were offered in exchange for a cure. John Paston, on his pilgrimage to Walsingham in the 14th century carried with him his weight in beeswax. With wax then at sixpence a pound

it was effectively a gift of at least four pounds and must only have been an option for the wealthy or desperate.

It was not just saints' shrines that were adorned with candles. From very early in the church's history candles had become associated with funeral rites. It was traditional for a bier to rest overnight in church surrounded by "mortars"—wax lights that were used specifically for funerals. By the 16th century it was common for the actual funeral to take place at night with an elaborate procession of candlelit mourners following the bier. The lavishness of the ceremony reflected the status of the dead person—it was important that no expense should be spared—and one of the key indicators of this was the number of mourners carrying expensive beeswax lights in the procession. On at least one occasion these wax tapers were sufficiently valuable for the entire procession to be "mugged" for their candles, as once happened at Stepney in East London.

❀ 65 ❀

Candle Users

Above: Amnesty International founder Peter Berenson relights the original candle in London to celebrate the 20th anniversary of the pressure group. The image of a candle flame burning within barbed wire became its logo.

Candles continued to be important long after the funeral had taken place. The saying of masses, reciting of prayers, and the lighting of candles over the tomb were essential ways to speed the passage of the medieval soul through purgatory. The far-sighted set up bequests while they were still alive to ensure that these rituals were carried out long after their actual death: a sort of medieval "afterlife insurance policy." In 1470 John Bracey, a "talaugh chanadler" left money in his will "for wax candles to burn round my tomb." His own tallow candles of course would have been of no benefit to his soul!

Most of these practices came to an end in England in the 1540s with the reformation of the church and dissolution of the monasteries. Candles were too closely associated with the rites of the Catholic Church and now had to go. The new prayer book dispensed with offices like Penance and Extreme Unction that all made heavy use of candles and forbade the use of holy candles, incense, elaborate vestments, and images of saints. Protestants and non-conformists continued to use candles as a source of light in their church services, but the mystical trappings of "sacramental magic" were gone. The lavish candelabra and candlesticks of churches and monasteries were either destroyed as "monuments of suspicion" or made ther way into private houses. "I can honour God as well with a fork full of muck as with a wax candle" was the robust response of one puritan at the time.

But simply banning or removing candles from religious services did not destroy the magical and votive associations that the church had allowed to build up over centuries. A considerable body of pre-Christian beliefs, fire magic, and sympathetic magic had become associated with candles alongside their use as religious objects and the two had uneasily co-existed within the pre-Reformation church and would continue to exist at the level of superstition and folklore long after.

Many religious festivals were already adaptations of an earlier ceremony or practice. Many of the winter festivals of lights practiced by faiths today that make use of candles—Jewish Chanukah, Hindu Diwali, as well as Christmas—derive from earlier light or fire festivals. In Italy Candlemas was substituted for the Roman Lupercalia, a festival of lights, while in England it replaced the Celtic fire festivals of Imbolc or Oimele. In northern Europe the Christian Church had to adapt various winter light festivals; in Sweden the lighting of candles on St. Lucey's Day of December 13, is a christianization of the start of the twelve day Viking fire ceremony of "Jol" that culminated in the burning of the "Yule" log on the hearth, itself the precursor of the Christmas tree.

"Holy candles," that had been blessed by the priest for use at the high altar, were stolen from churches to be used as charms because medieval superstition believed them to be objects with magical powers. They were used to protect farm animals or ward off sickness. According to one 16th century charm, candle ends left over from the ceremony of Candlemas had particular powers, "which lit in case of need would ward off danger in storms, hurt of frosts and hails and any devil's spite of fearful spirits." Magic was, of course, used for both good and ill and there are many accounts of candles being used to curse people. Like the one used in 1543 by Joanna Meriwether of Canterbury against a rival lover "for the displeasure that she bore towards a young maid named Elizabeth Celsay…made a fire upon the dung of the said Elizabeth; and took a holy candle and drop't upon the said dung. And she told the neighbours that the said enchantment would make the cule [buttocks] of the said maid divide into two parts."

The flickering and vulnerable candle flame was a very persuasive symbol of a human life or soul, and this inevitably found its way into various superstitions and folklore. It was an omen of death as in the guttering flame of a tallow candle with its "winding sheet" of solidified grease; or the flame could represent the dead, or soon to be dead, person's spirit as with the superstition of "corpse candles"—balls of flame seen in churchyards when someone had just died. The use of candles for the actual funeral accommodated several different pre-Christian beliefs: that the candle flames surrounding the corpse would keep out evil spirits; and that the flames would light the soul's journey to the underworld. This idea is also found in the Day of the Dead ceremony in Mexico. This conflation of Catholic Christianity and Aztec ancestor worship uses candles to light the way for the souls of the dead back to the hearth of their family for All

Left: Dewali candles produced in Burma for Hindu religious celebrations.

Right: Carriage candles were specially made to use in carriage lanterns.

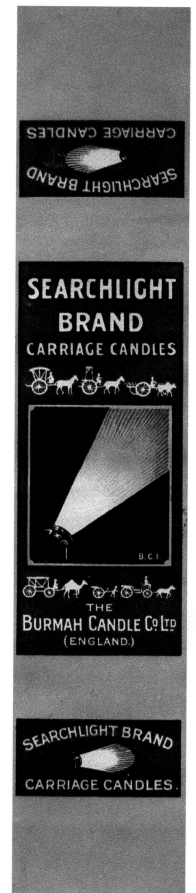

Candle Users

Left: An offering to the soul of a departed ancestor at a grave in a Japanese cemetery. The gift consists of carefully prepared food on a leaf and candles.

Below Left: A young boy offers candles and incense on the altar of a Buddhist temple in Myanamar, Burma.

Right: Many superstitions were attached to candle flames. Here a family looks in horror as a winding sheet of wax forms beneath the guttering candle flame. An old woman lies dying in the next room and the sheet of wax, representing the winding sheet she will be wrapped in in her coffin, confirms that her death is nigh.

Black magic and witchcraft were believed to get their powers from a deliberate reversal of Christian symbols. So black candles made of pitch that burned with a sinister blue flame—because of the high sulphur content—were an important part of medieval witchcraft. A 16th century French account describes witches worshipping the devil "each one holding a pitch candle of black wax in their hands." There are many local legends about devil candles, like that of Brother Thomas, the sacrist at Bromholm Priory, Suffolk in 1345. He was making a giant candle to be dedicated to St. Christopher, but the Devil corrupted him and the candle turned pitch-black. His penance was to carry the heavy black candle in his arms until it burned out; but miraculously he was forgiven and the candle slowly turned from black and became "as white as the lilies of the altar."

Across all cultures the candle, as an object that burned itself away, has been seen as a very potent symbol of mortality. The French expression *Il s'en alla comme une chandelle* (he went out like a candle) is used to describe a painless death. A local French wedding tradition that survived in both Alsace and Brittany would light two candles after a marriage. One candle represented the bride and the other the groom; whichever candle burned out first was supposed to predict which one of the couple would be the first to die. Another version of this sort of prediction was used by the early Byzantine churches in chosing a child's name; a number of candles were lit, each representing a possible name, and the child was given the name of the last candle to burn out. The

Souls Day. In the Catholic church excommunication was carried out "by bell and book and candle" and the snuffing out of the flame at the end of the ceremony symbolized that person's removal from the church.

For the Christian church the white color of bleached wax candles was an important part of their iconography. Their whiteness was visible evidence of their purity, just as the unbleached wax candles were only used for funeral services as a sign of mourning.

The Winding Sheet!

Design'd & Sketch'd on Stone by John Baker.

Printed by N, C.

Behold the candle! woeful sight!
A sheet is winding from the light!
        Pretending awful death;
An omen of the Lord's behest,
(As good old wives can well attest,)
        To all of mortal breath.

In ages past such tales arose,
(By Credence foster'd) to impose;
        And pious fraud enhance;
But more enlighten'd, we deride,
The absurd trash by dolts supplied
        As folly and romance.

Sketches of Character Pl.

benign pilgrim superstitions about "measured candles" and the use of wax for modeling images had precedents of immense antiquity. The ancient Egyptians used modeled wax figures called "shabti" to represent people in their tombs and for their magic. Enemies were modeled as a shabti, named, and then ritually burned. Wax lends itself to this kind of transference; it is easily sculpted and easily destroyed. Similarly in Voodoo and other occult practices a wax candle or figure is deliberately damaged or destroyed. There are many medieval Christian accounts of candles being used in this way. In 1490 a Johana Benet was accused of attempted murder after naming a candle after a man and using sorcery on it so that as it burned, he wasted away.

In the 17th century, with its hysteria about witchcraft, most of what today passes as magic was codified. The now traditional accoutrements of chalk circles, wands, sceptres, holy water, and candles were first defined then in books of magic. What is surprising is that at the end of the 20th century there is just as extensive a literature dedicated to "candle magic" and Wicca magic as practiced today, full of useful charms, spells, and candle recipes like that for Voodoo candles, which require goat's tallow that has been boiled for 13 minutes in rainwater.

Profane Light

"Well", said Jack. "I really think it will be worth doing. I've never been at the beggar's shop, and they say he lives well."

"Well, aye!" exclaimed his lordship; "fat 'o the land—dare say that man has fish and soup every day."

"And wax candles to read by, most likely," observed Jack, squinting at the dim mutton-fats that Baggs now brought in.

"Not so grand as that," observed his lordship, doubting whether any man could be guilty of such extravagance; "composites, p'raps."

Mr. Sponge's Sporting Tour J. S. Surtees, 1852

Artificial light was a resource that was not available to all. It was a luxury and in any society those at the top inevitably had more and better quality light. Back in Ancient Rome where homes were lit by the oil lamp, there was a simple arithmetic formula; the more wicks in your lamp, the brighter your light and the more important you were. Servants and slaves' lamps would only have a single wick while the lamps used by the family might have three or four. The truly poor lived in darkness.

Light had always been a prerogative of power. In many societies other people were used to hold the light; so torch or candle bearers became one of the trappings of power. Many different cultures used slaves in this way. In early Christian Ireland, in the seventh century the lord's "cumal" or female slave was required to dip a "cainnel" (candle) four hands breadth in length in lard or butter and to hold it in her hand to light the company at supper till they separated for bed. The tradition of bearing a light before a monarch continued into medieval Europe and was perpetuated by French kings into the 18th century when visiting princes and ambassadors were required to hold candles at the *coucher* of Louis XIV as a ritual humiliation. This idea survives in the expression "not fit to hold a candle to him."

The size of these early candles could have great significance. Irish kings had a "ri-chaindeal" or king candle burning all night outside their chamber, and the size of this candle—the length of a spear and thickness of a man's body—was a symbol of their power. These candles were even carried before the king when going into battle as when King Ossory attacked the Danes in AD 860 by night. A similar example of candles defining power and status was still found in Brunei in South East Asia in the 20th century. One of the prerogatives of the Bruneian ruling class was their right to burn candles during daylight—a good example of unnecessary and deliberately conspicuous consumption, and therefore only available to an elite. There were about 100 noble

Candle Users

Above: Candle lit society in the world of Jane Austen's novels—where the type of candles you burned defined your status.

either wax or tallow were extraordinarily significant. Aside from its use by the church, beeswax was the exclusive preserve of royalty, the aristocracy, and the very wealthy. Indeed, in some societies there was even less choice. The Irish *Book of Rights* stated that one of the prerogatives of the kings of Leinster was "to drink by the light of wax candles" at their palace at Dinree. By implication, the king's subjects were required to use lowlier forms of lighting.

Samuel Pepys, writing in his diary in the 1660s debated whether to buy beeswax candles and if the reduction in smoke would be worth the extra cost. In fact very few people could afford the three-fold to five-fold price difference. And even those that did choose to burn beeswax generally only did so when other people were looking! Even the wealthiest families alone at home might sit by the light of one or two tallow candles. And they would not stay up late. Unless you were entertaining then it was perfectly normal to be in bed before eight o'clock in the winter. In 17th and 18th century London court records show that many burglaries of peoples' homes were taking place as early as nine o'clock, because it was safe to assume that the householders would already be in bed and asleep.

By the 18th and 19th centuries wax candles were a defining and desirable object for the new middle classes. The highest quality wax or spermaceti candles might be on display in public rooms when entertaining; bedrooms, the kitchens, and servants' quarters would be provided with a decreasing quality of light as appropriate—bleached and molded candles, tallow dips, and rushlights. When guests came to stay at a country house party for an indefinite period, the candles provided for them in their rooms were used as a coded language for how long they should stay. If a guest went back to his room to discover the servants had replaced the wax candles with tallow ones, it was time to leave. In the same way the brightness of the light you provided was an easy

families in Brunei entitled to this honor and the size of their candles indicated their position in that aristocratic hierarchy; the sultan, of course, had the biggest, three feet high and weighing 12 pounds.

In northern Europe where olives did not grow and there was no good source of lamp oil the candle was the principal household light. The choice was between tallow and beeswax. In most European languages the two types of candle had different names—*chandelle* and *bougie* (French), *talglicht* and *kerze* (German). But in English a "candle" could be either wax or tallow. Even though the word allowed room for ambiguity the social implications of burning

Candle Users

metaphor for the warmth of your welcome. Burning large numbers of candles was, quite literally, conspicuous consumption and, more to the point, would be noted admiringly or enviously by your guests. In 1731 Robert Walpole, the former British prime minister, entertaining the Duke of Lorrain at his country house had 130 wax candles burning in the dining room and 50 in the saloon; such extravagant consumption was estimated to cost him 15 pounds per night. The writer William Beckford even used human torch bearers instead of candlesticks to light his guests as part of the Gothic extravaganza at his house Fonthill in 1801.

Jane Austen, writing in 1815 in her novel *Emma*, perfectly catches the anxieties about what the candles you burn say about you that were prevalent during her time. For example, Mrs. Elton describes Mrs. Bragge's house near Bath to Jane Fairfax,

"A cousin of Mr. Suckling, Mrs. Bragge…Everybody

was anxious to be in her family, for she moves in the

first circle. Wax candles in the school room! You cannot imagine how

desirable! Of all the houses in the

kingdom, Mrs. Bragges' is the one I would most wish

to see you in."

Wax candles in the childrens' school room would have been an example of monstrously conspicuous consumption—somewhat along the lines of gold plated taps in the bathroom today—and rightly Jane Austen is not sure who is the more vulgar, Mrs. Bragge for doing it or Mrs. Elton for being impressed by it!

The choice of candle may have had significance for the wealthy, but for the poor it was too often a choice between any sort of light or darkness. The peasant's experience of lighting in feudal Europe was mostly limited to the communal light he would occasionally share when he sat in his Lord's hall on feast days like Christmas and the Harvest Home. The rest of the time if he chose not to go to sleep with the sun then he sat in darkness.

In the more modern wage economies where laborers were no longer tied to the land and many earned their living as outworkers carrying on a trade in their own home, the ability to light your room and therefore continue working after sunset was crucial; it would directly affect just how much you earned. Some of the specialist silk weavers of Spitalfields in East London in the 18th century were able to have their houses converted with new large windows in their weaving rooms to shed the greatest amount of light over their detailed work, but most other trades did not earn enough to take such control over their working environment. Textile workers and hand loom weavers working from home in the Scottish High-lands were unable to work by the feeble glow of their peat fires; instead they would pool their money and buy a sack of expensively imported coals, by whose brighter light they might continue to work through the night. Even that was at least an improvement on the home knitters working in the woolen industry in the north of England. Frequently unable to afford fire or candle, they would sit in communal groups at one person's house in complete darkness knitting by touch and talking among themselves to make the oppressive blackness more bearable.

For really close work some means of delivering a bright light was essential. One early innovation was the "flash." Also known as the "Lacemaker's Condenser" this was a hollow, clear glass globe that was filled with water. When it was stood between a candle flame and the work that needed lighting it worked like a magnifying glass and increased the candlelight. It was fulsomely described by its maker in 1590 as being so powerful that "One candle will give a great and wonderful light, somewhat ressembling the sun's beames." As well as lacemakers it was used by engravers, jewelers, cobblers, clockmakers, and any other trades that needed bright light for detailed work.

From the beginning of the 18th century candles were heavily taxed in England. What started as a way of funding a European war remained a con-

Candle Users

venient source of income for the government that was periodically increased and not removed until 1831. Wax was taxed at three pence on the pound, tallow at one pence—effectively a 25 percent purchase tax. The only exemption was for rushlights made in the home; and it was this taxation that encouraged the return to rural rushlight making in the 18th century. While this was still possibly an option for country laborers, it was becoming less and less common. The political journalist William Cobbett, arguing for the repeal of candle tax in the 1821, regretted the demise of the rushlights of his childhood in favor of candles in laborers families. "Even if the labourer spent 15s a year on candles he would have to sit the greater part of winter evenings in the dark."

At least if you were employed as a domestic servant you received "bed, coals, and candles" as part of the standard contract; but the allowance was not always generous. As Jonathan Swift satirically suggests in his *Directions to Servants*, "Do all in the dark to save your Master's candles." At one large house, Woburn Abbey, in the 19th century each servant received just 14 candles a month in the summer and double that in the winter; while the staff working in the kitchen received half that allowance as they had the benefit of light from the kitchen fires. Manufacturers produced special "Servants Bedroom Candles;" the ones sold by Price's only lasted for half an hour. Unsurprisingly the candle-ends left in the dining room sticks at the end of the family's evening meal were a jealously guarded perk for servants, to be reused or sold on. There is an apocryphal story that Mr. Fortnum and Mr. Mason, two footmen in the court of Queen Anne at the beginning of the 18th century set up their now famous London shop with capital accumulated from the sale of such royal candle-ends.

Many people in the Establishment were actually quite happy for the poor to have restricted access to light. It was a part of the larger argument for not educating the lower classes. If you taught your workers and servants to read they might find out more than you wanted them too. And if they could read, perhaps it was better if they just sat in the dark after a full day's work rather than "improving" their minds with dangerous political or non-conformist ideas. Moral exhortations like "early to bed and early to rise" encouraged the laborer to do little with his life beyond his work. When groups of laborers did meet after work by candlelight it was often viewed with suspicion. Like the Norfolk parish priest who complained in 1805 about the spread of Methodist hymn singing in his village, "keeping the laborer and his family up at expense of fire and candle…until nine and sometimes later of a winter evening!"

As Britain became a more urbanized society fewer people had the time or materials to make their own light. Town dwellers were totally dependent on whatever prices were charged for poor quality tallow candles. Even a conservative paper like the *Illustrated London News* had to acknowledge by 1849 that there was a problem. On the one hand the poor were still limited to "offensive tallow with all its collateral disadvantages of guttering and spluttering, besides endless snuffing." While on the other,

"Those fortunate people inhabiting such terraces as Carlton Terrace and such squares as Grovesnor Square… had their wax and spermaceti lights, their portable gas-thermo lamps and glittering chandeliers, their girandole and carcel lamps in which they burnt huiles au naturel où parfumées, just as they pleased: and, what was better still, they had plenty of money to pay for these lustrous refinements."

In fact it was Victorian chemistry and industrial innovation that equalized things. The stearine candle of the 1840s and the paraffin candle of the 1870s were dramatically better lights than the tallow they replaced and yet were inexpensive enough to be available to all.

In the second half of the 19th century candles ceased to be the automatic choice of light for the

Candle Users

home. The wealthy could opt for the alternatives of oil lamps or gas light. Oil lamps were becoming cleaner and brighter while the new town gas was already the light of choice for street lighting and the work place and was beginning to be used in the home as well. In the 1860s the advent of kerosene as an inexpensive lamp oil coupled with new cheap improvements to lamps provided the poor with an alternative cheap bright light as well. It meant that there was almost no reason for anyone using candles any longer, unless from sentimentality or inertia. What is surprising is the extent to which people did in fact continue to use candles long after better alternatives were available.

In large country houses oil lamps and candles were used alongside one another in the 19th century, but had quite different functions. Candelabra and chandeliers were still used in drawing rooms, parlors, and dining rooms while the brighter oil lamps tended to be found in libraries, billiard rooms, halls, and passageways. It was a compromise between elegance and efficiency. Candles might not be as bright, but the centuries of investment in prestigious candlesticks and the status that these conferred was not lightly given up. The silver candlesticks were still under the particular care of the butler while the lower grade responsibilities for cleaning, filling, and trimming the oil lamps fell to the footmen.

Despite the obvious economic and technical benefits of gas, there was still opposition to its use in the home. Many people refused to use it, possibly as a reaction to its novelty. In 1852, when the House of Commons was being converted to gas, one elderly MP urged his fellow members "to return to the gentleman's light of good wax candles…which with handsome shades (green without and paler green within) would afford a pleasing and more efficient light." Even at the start of the 20th century many older people refused to make the transition and stuck with the lighting of their youth. The poet Swinburne, until his death in 1909, continued to work in his study at Putney by the light of three candles.

There was even a feeling among some of the upper classes that gas, because new-fangled, was necessarily vulgar. As a character in Benjamin Disraeli's novel *Lothair* put it, "He would not visit anyone who had gas in their home." When gas was installed—and use in Britain increased from two million homes in 1885 to seven million homes by 1920—it was still widely disliked because of the soot and pollution it created. The annual spring clean of ceilings and wallpaper darkened by the effects of gaslight was a very necessary ritual; and fresh coats of distemper had to be applied annually to the wall area below the cornice. Many houses would only have gas in halls and on stairs and continued to light living rooms using oil lamps and candles. And there was an almost total refusal to have gas in bedrooms.

When electricity became a viable alternative light there were similar initial reactions. Just as with the introduction of gas 40 years before, an older generation viewed the latest technology with suspicion. Once this extraordinarily bright electric light—the intensity of 80 candles—was available, there were concerns about its very brilliance and the effect upon the eyesight. "The electrician floods our rooms and streets with this eye poison" was one typical newspaper comment. The middle classes were anxious about just how to incorporate this new brightness into their room designs. From the 1890s, with the development of the inverted incandescent gas mantel and the vacuum light bulb, both electricity and gas were most commonly used in the home as suspended ceiling lamps. This downward lighting, flooding the entire room with an unaccustomed shadow-free light, was a novelty. Interior designers were now starting to have second thoughts about the intensity of the new lighting, suggesting that candles, unlike gas and electric light, gave "a comfortable and becoming clearness, sufficient to cheer but not

Candle Users

impertinently criticize." Overhead lighting, once the novelty wore off, was regarded as a bit common; the best households adopted lower wattage table lamps scattered about a room whose separate pools of light and surrounding shade recalled the gentle glow of preelectric days. There was almost a nostalgic yearning for the old times when the maid used to carry in the lamps or candles, draw the curtains, stoke up the fire and withdraw, leaving the family assembled round the hearth.

Candle makers happily exploited this nostalgia. As Price's catalog of 1909 put it "The peculiarly soft and kindly light given by candles, as contrasted with the painful glare derived from other sources, makes them eminently the light of the home circle and for domestic use."

Above: Candles were taxed in England from 1706 until 1831. It was a particularly bitterly resented tax as it affected the entire population. Wax candles were taxed at three pence the pound and tallow at one pence; effectively a 25 per cent purchase tax at contemporary prices.

Candles have been used for measuring time from at least the ninth century. The European tradition has the English King Alfred "inventing" the graduated candle clock, but there is clear evidence that the Chinese were using incense sticks and candles for time keeping at an even earlier date.

The Chinese incense clock and the English graduated candle worked on the same principle: candles or incense of a standard length and diameter will burn at a predictable rate and can thus be used as a simple measurement of time. Incense was laid out in measured lengths or coiled and suspended from a small frame where it burnt slowly without a flame. These clocks were already fully developed in China by the Sung dynasty (960-1279) when the technology was also introduced into Japan. They became more sophisticated with the introduction of a sequence of different fragrances so that those with sensitive noses could determine the time of day by the odor of the incense burning at a given moment. Incense clocks continued to be used locally in rural Chinese communities into the 20th century.

The English ascribe the invention of timed candles to King Alfred in the latter half of the ninth century. This is based on a single passage from a contemporary chronicler, Asser, who records that King Alfred: "commanded his chaplain to supply wax in sufficient quantity, and he caused it to be weighed in such a manner that when there was so much of it as would equal the weight of seventy two pence, he caused the chaplain to make six candles thereof, each of equal length, so that each candle might have twelve divisions marked across it." The six candles burnt in succession lasted 24 hours and each division indicated 20 minutes. The candles were used in a horn lantern to keep out draughts that would otherwise affect the burning time. Alfred had a reputation as a scholar king who divided his day into three equal portions of eight hours—for sleep, for government, and for prayer and study. The candle clock was supposed to have enabled him to do this. However, there is little evidence for its use beyond the royal palace.

If Alfred's experiments with timed candles did not appear to have caught on, there were still occasions when the use of candles could simultaneously provide light and give a rough approximation of time.

Above: Miners being lowered down a Cornish tin mine in the 19th century. Candles were important not just for the light they gave but also for giving the miners some idea of the length of time they had been working.

Candles were used extensively by miners up until the early 20th century; they were used in metal and ore mining and for coal mines where there was no risk of coal damp. An English coal miner in the Victorian period was always equipped with "A pound of pit candles and a clay candlestick," which would give him the three-fold benefit of light, a rough idea of the length of time he had worked, and, in extremis, an emergency food supply; the only benefit a tallow candle had over beeswax was that, as pure animal fat, it was edible.

The underlying principle of a substance's rate of burning being used as a measure of time was still a sound one. There was a later development in Britain in the 18th century which successfully used oil lamps. Lamps for use in bedrooms were marketed from 1730 in Britain fitted with a glass reservoir above the wick, graduated by hours and half hours. The falling oil level provided a reasonably accurate record of the passage of time and was lit up by the lamp below.

Another way in which candles were used to limit rather than measure time was in sales or auctions by candle. An item for sale could be bid for while a candle continued to burn; the last bid made before the flame went out—or before a pin inserted in the side of the candle fell out—purchased the goods. It was widely used for public auctions in France and England in the 17th and 18th centuries. In London the Navy Office auctioned off the hulks of redundant ships in this way, as described by Samuel Pepys in his diaries; in Liverpool it was used at public sales of slaves; in France it is still used to day for auctioning the vintage at certain vineyards. It also survives in some rural English parishes for the annual auction of the rental of parish lands to farmers more as a quaint local tradition.

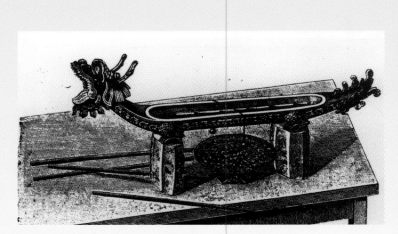

Above: A Chinese incense clock. The measured incense stick lay in the tray forming the body of the dragon. Weights on threads are laid across the incense stick at set points; the threads are burned through as the incense burns down and the weights fall onto the gong below, sounding the passage of time.

Street Lighting

The development of public street lighting is a confused mixture of religious procession, fears for law and order, and improvements to lighting technology. Candles and torches were used for nocturnal public ceremonies from at least the Roman period, and the development of street lighting derives, in part, from this festal or religious use. Constantine had the city of Constantinople lit up at night in the fourth century; but the motive was religious—it only took place on Christmas Eve and at Easter. In 13th century Paris every crossroads was illuminated by a burning torch, but again the principal purpose was religious, for a shrine was located at each crossroads and it was the statues of the Virgin Mary—not the occasional traveler's way—that was being illuminated. In medieval London the watch men were only issued with candle lanterns for use at night on Christmas Eve; then in 1405 this was extended to all saints' days.

Indeed, the very notion of traveling at night and needing light to do it by was viewed with suspicion at this time. Curfew—from the French *couvre feu*—applied in most towns and the carrying of candle lanterns and travel by night was generally forbidden. An early 14th century statute covering street lighting in London forbade any person from traveling after the curfew bell had tolled "unless he be a great man or other lawful person…having the warrant to go from one to another, with lanthorn in hand."

The stress on "lawful" is significant. Until street lighting was effective enough it was more attractive to the authorities to try and prevent any nocturnal activity, on the assumption that it was mainly criminal, rather than make it easier by street lighting. Early attempts at lighting in London were more to do with crime prevention than illumination, and the onus was on individual householders to display candle lanterns outside their house.

In 1415 all citizens were instructed to hang out such lights on winter evenings between All Hallows (November 1) and Candlemas (February 2). Later instructions limited this to putting out lights on "dark nights" defined as between the second night after a full moon and the seventh night after a new moon; they were required to burn from six o'clock until 11 the same night. Louis XIV of France introduced compulsory street lighting to Paris and then the rest of the country in the 17th century. In Paris this required 6,500 lanterns burning 1,625lb of candles a night. But even in the 1690s there was still a presumption that on moonlit nights, street lighting would not be required; in both Paris and London the lamps would only be lit for about 20 nights in each winter month—the rest of the time the moon was sufficient.

Part of the problem with street lighting was technical. It was initially difficult to get light to burn outside in wind and weather. *Flambeaux* and *cressets* burned vigorously and brightly and were well-suited to processions and events but were too short lived to provide practical lighting through the night. Candles, within the protection of a translucent horn lantern, were more economical, but glimmered dimly. By 1700 most European capitals were using oil lighting in their main streets—London, Vienna, Hamburg, and Amsterdam had all gone over. Predictably the candle makers of these cities complained about these attacks on their vested interests. In London the Tallow Chandlers Guild protested, "that the aforesaid lamps or lucidaries are merely novel and should they be encouraged they will cause many and much more intrusions upon other arts and mysteries." They were defending an impossible position and the "merely novel" oil lamps were soon, in turn, succeded. In 1809 London's Pall Mall became the first street in the world to be lit by gas. In 1878 and 1879 electric street lighting was introduced in Paris and London.

Left: Lamplighters in 19th century England.

Candle Users

3 Candlestick Makers

"You can conveniently stick your candle in a bottle, or with a lump of butter against the wainscot, in a powder horn, or in an old shoe, or in a cleft stick, or in the barrel of a pistol, or upon its own grease on a table, in a coffee cup or a drinking glass, a horn can, a teapot, a twisted napkin, a mustard pot, an inkhorn, a marrow bone, a piece of dough, or you may cut a hole in the loaf and stick it there."

Directions to Servants, Jonathan Swift, 1740

You cannot really use a candle without a candlestick. From the very earliest days the design of candlesticks and other ways of supporting lights was important. By the 15th century the craft of candlestick making was a recognized specialist trade. All sorts of other paraphernalia were produced over the centuries to improve the ways candles burned and were used. This chapter looks at the historical development of candle artifacts—candelabra, chandeliers and sconces, lamps and lanterns, snuffers, and save-all's and the way that candlestick design was incorporated into later lighting technologies like gas and electricity.

The earliest form of artificial light—the fire outside the cave—did not require containing within anything, but the development of lamps and candles meant ways had to be found of securing or supporting them. The pottery lamp of early civilizations was a self-contained unit that could be stood on any flat surface or even hung from the ceiling. Candles on the other hand, required some arrangement for supporting them upright. The earliest light holders were of course human. There are many accounts of primitive societies using servants or slaves as torchbearers or carriers of candles; the idea survives in the colloquial expression "Not fit to hold a candle to him." But such human candle holders were only available to rulers and were of course of limited use. While they might provide a magnificent illumination for a banqueting hall, you didn't necessarily want torch bearers in your bedroom. As artificial light ceased to be just the prerogative of wealth and power and became available to more people, so more practical ways of using candlelight in rooms had to be found.

There were two main methods of supporting candles that date from at least the Roman period—the "pricket" stick, which supported the candle on its base by impaling it on a spike and the "socket" stick, which sat the candle in a hollow socket. Numbers of socket sticks were found in the excavations of Pompeii; while in England a fine Romano-British example modeled as a horse with the socket in its back was excavated at Bath. However, most early medieval European candlesticks were prickets; they worked better for the larger wax candles and became associated with church and other public use from an early date. The socket candlestick tended to be used more in private houses; the hollow socket better contained the low melting point, smaller sized tallow candles that were burned in the home. Simpler domestic versions of the pricket candlestick were also found; sometimes no more than a block of wood with a spike hammered into it. Such crude supports were also used in smaller churches.

The best sticks, for the church, the royalty, and the wealthy were always made from metal. The earliest European centers of metalworking were the bronze foundries of Germany and the Low Countries who were manufacturing and exporting candlesticks from the tenth century; early examples of their craft survive in Hildesheim and Essen churches. Many surviving German candlesticks of this period use grotesque animal motifs: double-headed dragons, bears, and horses. A rare English example is the Gloucester Candlestick in the Victoria and Albert Museum. This is an elaborate gilt bronze candlestick, pierced and modeled with nude human figures fighting dragons among scrolls. It dates from 1104, when it was dedicated to the abbot of St. Peters, Gloucester. The Gloucester Candlestick clearly shows

Below: A Nigerian potter turns a clay candlestick on his simple foot-powered wheel.

Candlestick Makers

French silver candlesticks is supposedly because Louis XIV had them all melted down, using their bullion value to fund his European wars. But if silver had been the preserve of royal palaces in earlier centuries, it now started to replace base metals in wealthy Stuart and Georgian households for a huge range of household goods—cutlery, snuff boxes, toilet sets, drinking vessels, and most of all candlesticks. It was a highly reflective metal—when regularly cleaned and polished by servants—a quality that made it very suitable for light fittings and, when used in combination with fine beeswax candles, it was a compact and highly visible assertion of status and wealth.

"Take out of the way this pewter candlestick, which is so foule, make readie the silver candlestickes with the wax candles, for you knowe that she cannot endure the smell of tallow, because it doth most often stinke"

The French Garden, Peter Erondell, 1605

By the 18th century the best households would commission all their tableware from a silversmith as a piece. The designs of candlesticks matched the dishes, tureens, sauce boats, and condiment sets. In large houses brass candlesticks had already been banished to the passageways, servants quarters, and bed chambers.

The candlestick, whether it stood upon the table or was carried about the room, was only one of a number of ways of lighting a house. Wall mounted sconces or "candle plates" were popular from the 17th century. The sconce was a permanent fixture attached to the wall with a plate from which two or more branches supported sockets for candles. When possible these too were produced in silver so the highly polished wall plate behind the flames could serve as a reflector. A later refinement was the mirror sconce with a piece of looking glass substituted as the reflector. By the 19th century sconces were more

Above: Mirror sconces were an 18th century adaptation of the wall mounted sconce, with a looking glass behind to increase the illumination from the candle flame by reflection.

Below: Candlesticks in precious metals were always high status possessions. These comparatively modern ones were the gift of the Dominion of Canada to Prince Phillip and Princess Elizabeth upon their wedding in 1947.

PRICE'S CANDLES
WHICH WILL NOT DROP GREASE WHEN CARRIED.

generally known as girandoles which was the Italian name for any multibranched sconce or candelabra. To protect the wall decorations from the flame, glass smoke shades could be hung above the sconces to catch the sooty deposits. The sconce was used as a light fitting in a variety of ways. In the 17th century as wall fittings they provided illumination for long galleries and rooms. Chimney sconces were fitted either side of the fireplace. And they could also be attached to any appropriate piece of furniture.

There was an important relationship between the size and use of a room and the amount of candle lighting it would require. Big rooms needed more candles, but the use of the room was also a factor—public rooms like drawing rooms would be brightly lit, bedrooms could be gloomy. The actual construction and decoration of a room also had an effect on the amount of light. Developments in glass making in

Above: The traditional chamber or flat candlestick for use in bedrooms remained basically unchanged for two centuries. It was designed to be carried easily upstairs upon retiring for bed. The non-drip candles are a reference to the introduction of plaited wicks after the 1840s that did away with the problems of candles guttering and needing snuffing.

the 17th and 18th centuries allowed rooms to receive much more sun. The replacement of small casement windows containing many small panes of leaded glass by the large single sheets of glass used in sash windows made an enormous difference to daytime light levels and helped create an expectation for better light at other times. Furnishings, wall finishes, and color schemes could all help lift the level of light that candles gave off. It was calculated that a wainscotted room of a standard size would need six candles to light it where the same room in a stucco finish would need eight; the varnished wood being more reflective

Candlestick Makers

Above: From the 18th century candles were frequently mounted on a piece of furniture like the sideboard here with a large glass behind to reflect the light back into the room.

whist as well as billiards and music recitals. The general growth of literacy and the fashion for needlework and watercolor among women also created demands for better light. One important social change was in the time at which people ate their main meal; the dinner hour moved forward from the afternoon to the evening as the century progressed, so more light was needed to eat by, particularly in winter. Single socket candlesticks were insufficient and gave way to candelabra with two, three, or even four branches. Some surviving early 18th century sticks have had additional branches fused on at a later date showing how the fashion for better lighting at the dinner table grew.

Furniture to support and display this increasing armory of light fittings became a necessity. The uncluttered rooms of the Middle Ages sometimes contained candle niches constructed in their deep stone walls to stand a light on. As furniture became more common in houses, so there were more points to place candles. By the 18th century a whole sub-genre of candle furniture had built up. The most important of these, the *guèridon* or candle stand, was a small table specifically for supporting candlesticks or candelabra. The name comes from the French term for a black servant or page boy, and many of the 17th century *guèridon* were indeed sculpted African figures supporting a tray, which served as the table top. These were imported to England and were known by the now racially offensive term "blackamoor stands." Taller tripod mounts for candles were known as *torchères*. Sheraton, the furniture designer noted in 1793 that "candle stands are used in drawing rooms for the convenience of affording additional light to such parts of the room where it would be neither ornamental nor easy to introduce any other kind." In other words they provided a flexible and highly elegant way of extending the lighting beyond that provided by fixed wall sconces and chandeliers.

than the matt plaster. The 18th century Earl of Hardwicke deliberately chose to have his living room at Wimpole Hall painted in an expensive French White, rather than the standard Ash or Olive Grey; not simply because the white was more fashionable color but rather because of the savings made on lighting; his wife calculated that they would only now require two instead of four candles to light the room.

Wall mounted sconces that had worked so well in the long galleried rooms of Stuart houses started to go out of fashion in the 18th century; they gave a general light to the edge of the room, but did not illuminate the center. People started to have higher expectations and were no longer prepared to sit in the near-dark. There were requirements for portable, direct lighting to illuminate newly fashionable evening pursuits—table games like ombre, looe, and

Another approach adopted by cabinet makers was to attach candle sconces to appropriate pieces of furniture. Such "conveniences for candles" were fitted to anything that might be used for close work. Mirrors and cheval glasses were popular because of the way the sconces could reflect light back into the room. Writing tables, library chairs, and pianos obviously benefited from candles close at hand and were similarly equipped. Other pieces of furniture like bureaux, card tables, and bookcases often had "candle boards" or "candleslides" fitted; these were extendable wooden trays that could be pulled out to stand a candlestick upon as required. Bigger pieces of furniture that required large amounts of light might have a dedicated ceiling fitting; the hanging lights placed above snooker and pool tables in pubs and pool halls today are a direct descendant of the chandeliers used in country house billiard rooms in the 18th and early 19th centuries. Upstairs, in the aristocratic dressing room, a pair of simple candle stands with shorter candlesticks stood either side of the mirror and dressing table; this was the "toilet set." In less wealthy bedrooms this was replaced by the "triad"—a simple composition formed by a table, mirror, and candlestick—which alongside the bed and the closet stool or chamber pot might well be the only furniture in the room. In the poorer respectable households these arrangements could be very minimal indeed, as Bella Wilfer complains to her sister who she shares a cramped bedroom with in *Our Mutual Friend*,

> "You needn't stand between me and the candle for all that…This is another of the consequences of being poor! The idea of a girl with a really fine head of hair having to do it by one flat candle and a few inches of looking glass."

As well as being the place for sleep the bedroom was also synonymous with sexual activity, and thus the candlestick beside the bed became associated in peoples' minds with lust. In 17th century Dutch art, in paintings like Jan Steen's *Woman At Her Toilet*, a bedside candlestick and the chamber pot were both rec-

Above: Vauxhall night lights of the 1850s.

Below: An elaborate Georgian cut-glass chandelier in the drawing room of a stately home.

Candlestick Makers

ognized motifs or visual clues for prostitution, debauchery, and lust, informing the viewer about the subject of the painting.

The particular requirements for light in the bedchamber—a room that you only came upstairs into when it was already dark—prompted the development of the portable "chamber candlestick"—also

Below: New patent night light label from the 1850s; the palm tree on the label is a reminder of the source of the wax—from palm and coconut oil.

known as "flat candlestick"—with a broad pan, short stick, and carrying handle. Early designs with their wide bases and long handles resembled nothing so much as a frying pan. These were followed by more compact sticks with ring handles, often incorporating a detachable candle snuffer and a conical extinguisher. These lightweight chamber sticks were much more portable than the cumbersome oil lamps; they were easier to carry up stairs and simpler to light and extinguish. The bedroom was the last room in the house to go over to gas light. Most Victorians were too anxious about the dangers of poisonous fumes and poor ventilation to have it where they slept. As a result, most homes continued to use chamber candles into the 20th century when they were finally replaced by electric light.

By the 18th century fashionable candlestick design was becoming incorporated into the overall design of room settings. Candles and candlesticks were now much more of a decorative component within a room, no longer just a functional source of light. Attention was paid to the look and effect of candle lighting in the same way that we use electric light and light fittings today as a part of the total interior design of a room. The plain style of Queen Anne was superceded by the more elaborate work, especially of the Adam brothers, that was fashionable from the 1750s. They were responsible for introducing the motifs of contemporary furniture into candlesticks—the stick now became a fluted neo-classical column, the socket was an urn-shaped container that recalled classical models, while the beaded molding round the base of the candlestick was the same as the decorative detail found on furniture. The paraphernalia of candle lighting was now part of a larger design brief.

The ultimate in designed candle lighting was of course the chandelier. Suspended from the ceiling and containing anything up to 50 candles they served quite literally as a dazzling reminder that bright light was still the preserve of wealth and power. Initially they were only ever to be found in

Candlestick Makers

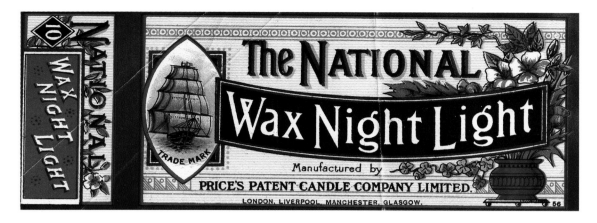

palaces, cathedrals, or mansion houses (the earliest surviving chandelier is in Aachen cathedral and dates from 1168) because these were the only places appropriate for such a costly and ostentatious form of light. Less elaborate brass and carved wooden chandeliers started to be found in wealthy homes from the 15th century; a recognizable brass example can be seen in Jan Van Eyck's painting of the *Arnolfini Marriage* with finial at the top, a globe at the base, and tiers of branches supporting candle sockets.

The most costly chandeliers were made of solid silver or—possibly even more desirable—of rock crystal. This was expensively imported from Venice or Bohemia and produced dazzling effects of reflected light. By the 1720s the most fashionable people aspired to the slightly less expensive, though equally reflective, lead glass chandelier. These appear to have developed from the earlier fashion for mirror sconces and, like them, were the work of looking glass makers rather than candlestick makers. The taste for these peaked later in the century when these chandeliers were festooned with vertical chains of cut glass droplets, so the whole ensemble looked like a glittering tent. Perhaps the most extravagant was the chandelier commissioned by the then Prince of Wales for the drawing room at Carlton House. 56 candles were suspended below a tent of 30 chains, each threaded with 30 cut-glass, 16-faceted drops of different sizes. The whole ensemble even in 1808 cost 1,000 guineas.

A chandelier was a peculiarly extravagant way of lighting a room. The actual chandelier was exquisite, expensive to purchase, and equally expensive to maintain. It was unusual for a large house to have

Candlestick Makers

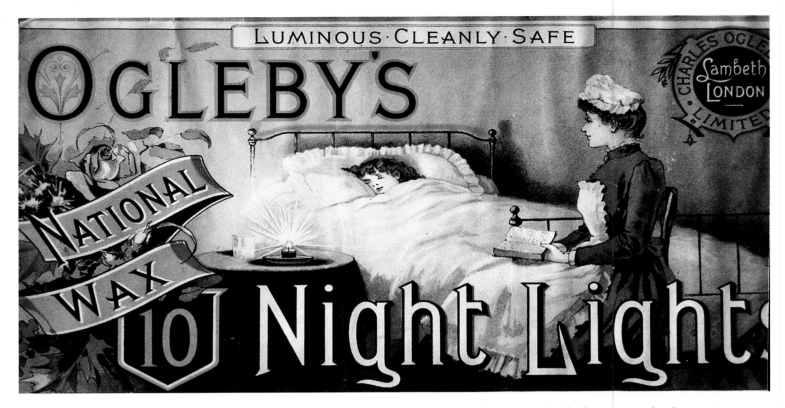

LUMINOUS · CLEANLY · SAFE

OGLEBY'S

NATIONAL WAX

[10] Night Lights

CHARLES OGLEBY
Lambeth LONDON
LIMITED

Above: Long after other types of candle had fallen from use, the night light continued to have a function. Because it was a stable, safe light there was less of the fire risk associated with a night light and it became connected in the public's mind with children's bedrooms and sick rooms where it was also used for warming food.

more than a matching pair—one for the hall and one for the ballroom. Not only did it consume large numbers of candles, it also required a huge amount of servant's time to maintain it in use. When illuminated it undoubtedly looked wonderful, but it epitomized all the drawbacks of candles. It was the least spontaneous form of lighting; the servants had to lower it on pulleys to clean and fill it with candles. The simultaneous lighting of anything between 15 and 50 candles was time consuming. Some houses experimented with threads dipped in sulphur linking up each candle with a fuse, but this was little more than a messy party trick—the burned up fuses dropped onto the guests below and spoiled their clothes. Chandeliers by implication had to burn the finest wax candles; the logistics of having to lower and snuff tallow candles every half hour was out of the question. It was also a less efficient way of light-

ing a room because the light was so high up. A room that could be lit by six or eight table mounted candles would need at least ten ceiling mounted lights to have the same effect.

Given all this it is no surprise to find that when the duchess of Portland received King George III at her home in 1779 and she had the chandelier in the hall lit in his honor, it was the first time it had been lit for 20 years. For many households it was just too much effort and expense. Another problem with chandeliers was the immense amount of heat that these lights would generate. At the coronation of King George IV in 1820 the combination of 28 large chandeliers and a huge number of people in an unventilated space caused the candles to melt and drip hot wax on the guests below. Candles also used up a huge amount of oxygen, the flame was reckoned to use the same amount as two people, so that candle-lit rooms would quickly became airless, stifling spaces. The swooning heroine of the Victorian novel—that cliché of romantic fiction—was as much a victim of de-oxygenated rooms as she was prey to her own emotions. The Jewish writer Israel Zangwill,

Candlestick Makers

PRICE'S PARTILITES

Above: This 1950s label tries to inject a little party spirit into a by now rather staid product.

described a similarly airless East London synagogue in the late 19th century; "the room was badly ventilated, and what little air there was generally sucked up by a greedy company of wax candles, big and little, stuck in brass holders."

The manufacture of Sheffield plate starting in the 1760s was an important development; it provided the middle classes with the illusion of solid silver for their candlesticks and other household goods, but at between a third and a fifth of the price of the real thing. Sheffield plate was a sandwich of copper sheet between two thinner layers of silver and became a popular material for candlesticks; it had the look of silver without the weight or cost. When Horace Walpole purchased a pair of such sticks for two guineas, their solid silver equivalent cost ten guineas; the same design in brass would have cost about 12 shillings. By the middle of the 19th century Sheffield plate was superceded by electroplating, which was again used extensively for candlesticks.

While most people in Europe used candles for their domestic lighting only a tiny percentage of those populations had access to silver sconces and glass chandeliers. The fine distinctions between solid silver, Sheffield plate, and electroplated silver were meaningless to 90 percent of them. Even the relatively humble brass candlestick was a luxury item.

It may have been commonplace in middle class homes, but it was not likely to feature in either the cottage of the rural laborer or the tenement of the factory worker.

In the Middle Ages it had been common for "persons of importance to have their candles fixed on silver stands while ordinary people had them fixed on loaves of bread cut up into trenchers." Although almost no medieval silver sticks survive, the base metal candlesticks that did survive were still exclusive items that had been produced for the church and the aristocracy. For the rest of society the candlesticks that were produced for ordinary domestic use tended to be manufactured from available and easily worked materials—fired clay, turned wood, locally forged iron, and carved bone were all used. And these household goods—functional objects whose sole purpose was to hold a candle upright while it burned—were not valued or preserved. Where they have survived it is often only as archaeological finds and fragments. In southern England quantities of green glazed earthenware sticks with bell shaped base, short stem, and long outward tapering socket have been found on medieval sites.

Many people couldn't even afford the candle,

never mind the stick to burn it in. One solution was to make their own tax-exempt rush lights. These long, fragile tapers had to be supported in a special device that held them while they burned. The iron rushlight holder had a simple pair of jaws that clamped on the rushlight and held it at an angle of 45° to the vertical; a couple of inches was drawn through at a time, otherwise the rush would bend under its own weight. The rushlights one technical advantage over the tallow candle—that it did not require snuffing—was outweighed by the greasy ash deposit it let fall to the floor as it burned up. As a result these lights were only ever used in the stone or earth-floored country cottage with no pretensions to furnishings. For the same reasons, rushlight holders were never mass produced by urban metal workers and candlestick makers. It seems they were always made locally to order by village blacksmiths from wrought iron. The surviving examples show a large degree of variation on the basic design; some were table or floor standing, others wall mounted or ceiling hanging; many incorporated a socket candlestick as well. They were functional, unornamented pieces of household equipment.

When it came to producing metal candlesticks for ordinary people these also tended to be of iron that could be worked locally. Crude wrought-iron, single socket sconces and chamber sticks were made with spikes on the end to be hammered into a wall beam; there would not have been very much furniture to stand a candlestick on. The technique of drawing out a tube in iron to make the hollow stick was beyond the skills of a local smith; as an alternative, column candlesticks could be made from a thin flattened strip of iron wound to form a hollow spiral. Pewter, an alloy of tin and lead, was an expensive metal until the 16th century. But as first brass and then silver became the fashionable metal for candle-

sticks, pewter became the cheaper alternative for poorer people, used for candlesticks, teapots, mugs, plates, and cutlery. By the 18th century pewter started to be replaced by tin plate. This was a new process that coated sheet iron in tin to make an inexpensive, rustproof, and easily worked metal. Tinplate candlesticks and candle lanterns continued to be made and sold into the 20th century and remained the cheapest way of burning candles, less expensive even than the enameled and japanned ironware that also started to be produced. By 1850 a tinplate chamber candlestick cost just sixpence, the same price as a pound of cheap tallow candles.

Potentially cheaper still was the night light or "mortar." (The name derives from its use to light funeral biers in churches.) This was a self-contained cylinder of wicked wax in a paper or metal wrapping that had the advantage of not even requiring a candlestick. It could be safely stood on a plate or dish with a little water in the base and because it was also more stable it was less of a fire risk than a candle. This was the most popular, because inexpensive, source of lighting for the 19th century urban poor. Price's, was producing 32 million night lights a year by the 1870s. They were also popular in middle class households where they were generally concealed within special night light holders. Various elegant porcelain and pottery designs exist from the Regency period. The U.S. and English manufacturer Samuel Clarke produced a dazzling range of "Fairy Light" holders in colored and etched glass that were briefly fashionable at the end of the century. He even attempted to compete with gas lighting by producing conversion kits for gas chandeliers that replaced each single gas burner with a triple fairy light holder. At the beginning of the 20th century the night light moved upstairs to the children's bedroom. Suitably hidden within a brightly colored holder—anything from Noah's Ark to a

Right: The potential market for children's candles was discovered from the 1930s and a whole new range of candle products, including early examples of cinema merchandising, were produced to tap it.

Candlestick Makers

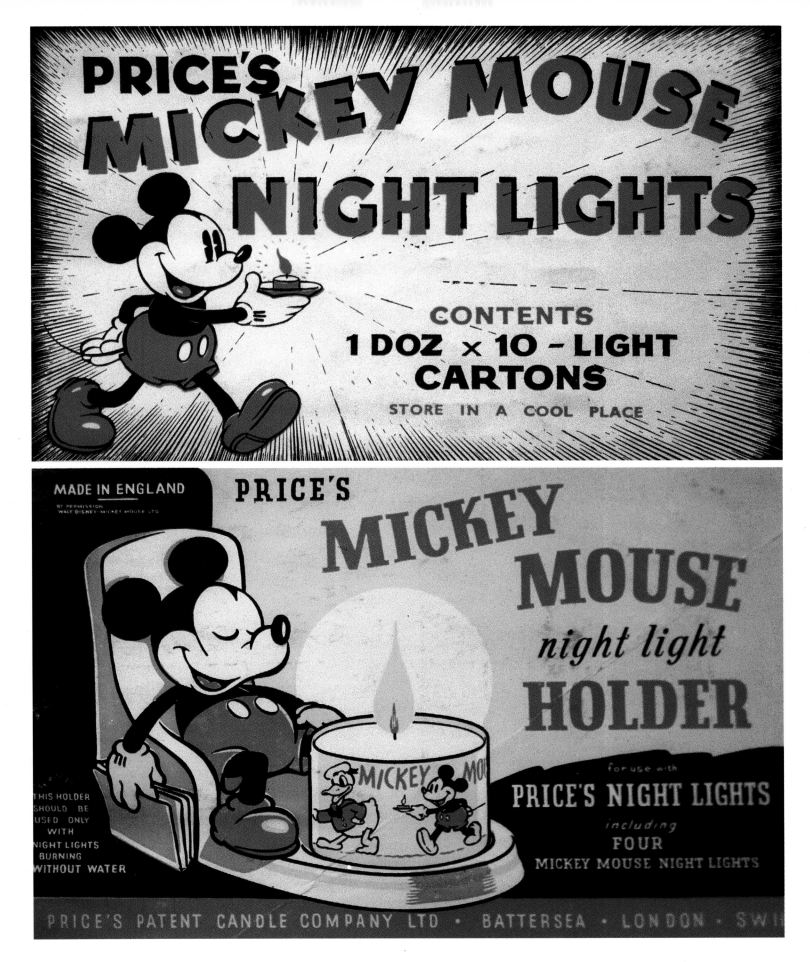

Candlestick Makers

Walt Disney character—it provided a safe and reassuring low-level light through the night until the advent of low-wattage bulbs provided a more convenient alternative.

How did you take the rather delicate candle flame and allow it to be used out of doors? The candle lantern was one way of protecting the candle from draughts and rain and providing a weatherproof light. A cylinder or box of thin metal with a vented roof to give air to the flame was easily produced; the technical problem was finding a sufficiently robust yet transparent fire-proof material for the flame to shine through. The "dark lantern" was one way to solve the problem; it completely enclosed the flame and had a door at the front that could be opened as required to cast light, but it meant the rest of the time the user was literally in the dark. The first solution was the "lanthorn" or "horn lantern," which used fine slices of treated cow horn as a transparent, fireproof pane. When these slices were boiled the horn became translucent. Unlike glass, horn was locally available and easy to produce. It only gave a faint light but it provided a weatherproof surround for the candle and was much used by watchmen and by farmers. Its advantage in farm buildings was that it was less likely to get knocked over and cause a fire. From the 16th century lanterns started to be made with glass, but the earliest thick green leaded glass was scarcely any more transparent than the horn. The candle lantern was always a strictly functional piece of lighting equipment; however, more elegant brass wall-mounted lanterns were sometimes used in large houses to provide background lighting for draughty areas like stairs and passages. Tinplate and japanned candle lanterns continued to be manufactured for

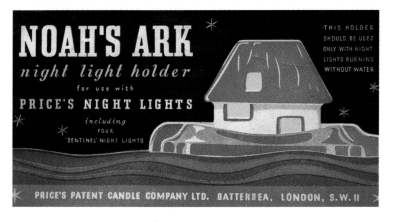

Above: This comforting Noah's Ark children's night light holder dates from the 1930s.

farm and camping use into the 20th century.

Back inside the house, candle screens were used to protect the flame from draughts and to protect the eyes from glare if people were doing close work by candlelight. Such screens took several forms; there were freestanding frames of translucent fabric or paper that could be placed between the flame and the draught; or cylindrical surrounds that the candle was placed within; portable bedroom chamber sticks that were regularly carried along draughty passages were improved with glass cylindrical shades over the candle. Shades as used today on table lamps—a conical opaque cover above the lamp—developed from the candle screen. Candle lamps were being produced from the late 18th century for use in the office and for reading at home; they used a shade to direct the light down onto a book or papers. The main difficulty was how to support the shade above a candle that was changing its height as it burned down. Various inventions for keeping the shade company with the descending flame were produced. These included ratchets that allowed the shade to descend with the candle or ejectors within the stick that allowed the candle to be pushed up as it burned down. The most successful of these was a spring-loaded candle lamp, patented in the 1840s and then fairly universally adopted. The candle was inserted in a metal tube with a pierced domed top through which the wick could burn; the spring in the base kept the candle pushed against the top of the tube, the flame remained at a constant height and elegant colored and opaque glass shades, mimicking the aesthetics and design of oil lamps, could be securely attached to the metal tube.

A significant development from this was the

carriage lamp. When the spring loaded candle lamp was enclosed in a glazed metal lantern with a polished reflector then it could be used outside like a lantern. Fitted onto horse drawn vehicles, burning a special hard, high-melting point candle the carriage lamp was a very successful form of candle lighting that remained in use up to the early 20th century. Smaller versions were produced for bicycles and they were only made obsolete when brighter portable lighting, first by acetylene and then by electric batteries, replaced them.

There were various other items of candle paraphernalia that every household, however poor, would have used. The *guèridons*, shades, and candle stands might have been exclusive to the refined world of the upper classes, but even the poorest house needed certain basic equipment to burn candles properly. As Swift wrote in the 1720s, "A Candlestick, Snuff dish and Save-All, And thus his Household Goods you have all."

The "save-all" was a device for burning up candle ends; it usually took the form of a small cup with some means for securing the candle-end—a pricket or wires. There were many superstitions about letting a candle burn out in its socket; it was supposed to bring bad-luck; and on a more practical level it filled the socket with messy congealed tallow and made it harder to put the next candle in. Early socket sticks often had a hole through the side of the socket to make it easier to extract the candle end. By the 18th century these were largely superceded by socket ejectors built into the hollow stem of the stick; a sliding knob enabled you to push out the candle-end. In

all households the value of these ends was recognized. In wealthy houses they might be the perk of the servants, but for ordinary people they constituted an additional source of light that they could not afford to waste. Hence the "save-all."

The "snuff dish," "snuffers," or "candlesheres" was an essential item until the development of the snuffless candle. Even the humblest household needed to trim their candle wicks. Snuff was the burned portion of the wick that remained in the candle flame and caused the light to dim and the candle to drip grease or gutter. By trimming the snuff the candle burned brightly again; it was an operation that ideally had to be carried out every 30 minutes. Snuffers were basically a pair of specially adapted scissors. They had a small semicircular dish attached to the larger blade that caught the still smouldering wick so that it did not fall and damage the furnishings.

Not only have snuffers disappeared—they were instantly rendered obsolete in the 1840s—but so too has the original meaning of to snuff. When we use the term "to snuff a candle" today what we really mean is to snuff out, that is to put it out. Swift, in his *Advice to Servants* provided a long and facetious list of ways of putting or snuffing out a candle, including the suggestion "when you go to bed, after you have made water, you may dip the candle end into the chamber pot." Most servants and their masters and mistresses appear to have preferred either the "douter" or the extinguisher to their chamber pot. The douter, like the snuffers, was a modified pair of scissors with turned flattened ends that squeezed the wick and put out the flame. The extinguisher was a metal cone, like a witch's hat that could be placed over the flame. Either system was preferred to blowing the candle out which caused the room to smell of the burning snuff and was likely to spatter molten wax or tallow.

The candlelit houses of previous centuries had other supporting paraphernalia. Candle boxes in tin plate or japanned metal were wall mounted in rooms to store the candles in. Prior to the development of

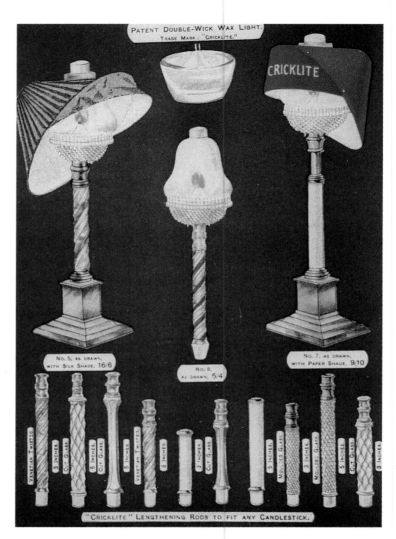

Above and Right: Candle companies like Clarke's and Price's aggressively promoted shade candle lamps in the early 20th century; their selling point was the gentle down light that they gave in contrast to the harsher glare of electricity.

the phosphorous match and instantaneous light in the 1840s the actual means of lighting the candle was an issue. Most houses would have used tinder boxes, striking a flint against metal to raise a spark. Some of these boxes conveniently had a candle socket attached to transfer the flame to. Wax tapers were generally used for lighting candles, and a taper holder was often attached to the backof a conical extinguisher on a pole, providing a dual purpose tool for lighting and extinguishing chandeliers.

The introduction of new lighting methods saw many existing light fittings converted. Fine chandeliers were either piped for gas or wired for electrici-

Candlestick Makers

ty, oil lamps were converted for gas; later on gas fittings were rewired to take electric light. These short term conversions were a mixture of economy and sentiment. But gas and electric light fittings continued to be informed by the designs of earlier candle lights and oil lamps long after they had fallen from general use. Chandelier designs were reworked for the new gasoliers and electroliers. The standard "S bend" or "swans' neck" wall-fitted gas lights derived directly from the candle sconces of the 17th century. Electric table lamps of the 1890s were supported by the fluted columns of the previous century's candlesticks or the glass and metal bases of paraffin oil lamp; with their white glass shades and brass fittings only the intensity of their light and the tell-tale flex betrayed what they really were. One can still trace the residual lamp-oil reservoir in the spherical base of many table lamp designs today. By the 1890s household furnishings catalogs were already offering "electric light bulbs to represent the flame of a candle" and polished brass Louis XVI-style wall lights wired for electric light. In the Edwardian revival of period furnishings associ-ated with the Arts and Crafts movement the Georgian candle sconce was recast for electricity in brass and steel by designers like Ernest Gimson. More populist versions, tricked out with dummy candles complete with ridges of realistic wax, surmounted by the "flame" of small filament light bulbs are with us today, though now flickering on the borders of kitsch.

The emphasis of large scale lighting design and factory manufacture shifted inexorably from oil lamps and candle fittings to concentrate first on gas and subsequently just electric light. Some cheap japanned metal and tinplate candlesticks continued to be produced—with their distinctive broad base, carrying handle, and short stick they were a direct throwback to the 18th century brass chamber candlestick. But these were now utility items of last resort, to be looked out of cupboards when the electrics fused or the gas meter ran out. Quality candlestick manufacture in the early 20th century became the preserve of the specialist craftsman, often working in precious metals for an increasingly exclusive market. The Art Nouveau silver work of the Danish designer Jensen; the popular Art Deco ceramics of Clarice Cliff with her garish oranges and greens and cubist influenced forms; the 1950s "Contemporary" designers from Italy and Scandinavia using stainless steel, glass, and aluminium; the new craft silversmiths of the 1960s and 1970s like David Mellor and Robert Welch; all of these 20th century designers have revisited and redefined the candlestick How- ever as candlesticks became increasingly "designed" they also lost their functionality. Not only was there less need to burn candles for their light, but as they became increasingly exquisite artifacts —an existing form within which an artist could explore a design— there was an in-creasing reluctance to use them for anything other than their ornamental value.

GRAND PRIX
PARIS 1889.

Candlestick Makers

4 Candle Making Today

Even as recently as the 1960s the candle business still seemed to be in terminal decline. Consumption was falling year on year. Small, limited niche markets still remained for church candles, art candles, and for the social needs of the middle classes—candles for flower arranging, table settings and dinner parties. But there were few new products and almost no investment. Aside from birthday cakes and Christmas, candles for most people meant the white household candles and night lights to be found tucked away on the bottom shelves of grocers and iron mongers: awkward reminders of a recent past, not quite obsolete, certainly not yet quaint. In England they were still too closely associated in peoples' minds with the austere years of the Second World War and the rationing of the 1950s—emergency lighting for air raid shelters during the Blitz or in the electricity shortages of the post-war years. They were the light of last resort that came out of the cupboard for power cuts, miners' strikes, and other crises. In the newly enriched Britain of the Sixties, in "the white heat of the technological revolution" when suddenly everything was available on the shelves again, no one needed to be reminded of that recent past or expected to have to be still burning candles.

But by the 1990s the position of candles had changed out of all recognition. People were burning increasing quantities in the home and for an extraordinary number of new and different purposes; the status of the once humble object had been transformed. Specialist candle shops were opening in the smallest towns. Supermarkets who had once tucked a few boxes of white household candles away with the shoe polish and disinfectant now had bright, displays of candles in prominent places in their stores. The candlestick and night light holder, in all their myriad post-modern variety were becoming desirable art objects once more, to be found in a bewildering range of designs and materials in even the smallest gift shop. The color, shape, size, and scent of candles knew no limit as candle makers produced more designs and novelty ideas for a market seemingly without limit.

Candles started to be burned for more reasons than ever before. As soon as everyone had equal access to electric light the old arguments about one type of light for the rich and one for the poor no longer applied; there was no longer anything shameful or inadequate about candlelight when every body had 100 watt bulbs in their rooms. Instead it was able to become distinctive, ambient and sophisticated. Candlelight was softer, kinder on the eyes, more elegant, and somehow more artistic than the

Right: "Beeswax" pillar candles; originally produced for church use, these percentage wax candles are now equally popular in the home. Although they contain as little as ten percent beeswax this is still sufficient to have an effect on their burn time and their fragrance.

Candle Making Today

Above: A nurse cares for a baby by candlelight in a London hospital during "the Winter of Discontent"—the energy disputes and power cuts of December 1970 that saw most of England looking in its cupboards for its old stocks of candles.

Left: Bank clerks in 1947
working through a power cut
by candlelight.

Below: Post-war candle-power
lights baby in the bath. A London
family in 1947 resort to candles
and oil lamps during one of the
many power cuts at this time.

Above: Candles for celebration; model swans, illuminated by more than 6,000 candles float across a pool in Lititz, Pennsylvania as part of that town's July 4 celebrations in 1955.

undiffused glare of electricity; candlelit rooms became spaces that conveyed a recognized mood, for dining, for listening to music, for relaxing.

Part of the enduring charm of the candle is its historical associations. We live in an age that has become more interested in the "heritage" of our past than any previous one has been. The candles that we purchase today to burn are to all intents and purposes the same as those burned by our ancestors 100, 200, or 400 years ago. They provide us with a tangible link with that past and lend themselves to our end-of-century fascination with things historical. Very few people are operating at the extreme level of obsession as someone like Dennis Severs, an American who has turned his Georgian house in Spitalfields, East London into a miniature 18th century theme park, lit totally by candlelight and providing period costume tours of the house to tourists. But that is just one extreme of the 1980s and 1990s enthusiasm for restoring and recreating period homes. The obviously "retro" qualities of traditional candle shapes and designs still contain a

strong historical appeal. Wax candles and candlesticks are there on the mantelpieces of many carefully recreated Victorian houses, above the reinstated cast iron fireplace and set off agreeably by the William Morris wallpaper, the Liberty print curtains, and the period furniture.

This interest in the historical qualities of the candle has been followed up by the manufacturers with various attempts to return to traditional raw materials and to revive and repackage the candle as a heritage product. At a time when consumers are also questioning the use of fossil fuels and seeking a greener alternative to paraffin wax this is not merely playful historicism. There is a growing interest in candles that can support alternative lifestyles.

Beeswax is one such material that has been reintroduced for general use. Until the 1990s beeswax candles were produced almost exclus-ively for the Catholic and Anglican churches by specialist church candle makers. But recently they have had a new lease of life. Successfully marketed for use in the home, the combination of old fashioned raw material and the simple, traditional design of the pillar candle means that they are now just as likely to be found on the dinner table as on the altar. Consumption has doubled over the last five years although the quantity actually supplied to churches has remained unchanged—the growth in sales has come purely from candles used in the home. The age old problem with beeswax is still the same as it was 500 years ago; it is just so expensive compared to the alternatives and pure beeswax candles would be just too expensive. As a result "Beeswax Church Candles" as sold for domestic use today rarely contain more than 10-15 percent actual beeswax. Even the true church candles made for religious use now only contain 20-25 percent beeswax. The 100 percent pure beeswax candle is a rare bird, nowadays glimpsed only occasionally at state funerals and royal marriages. Even ten percent beeswax makes

Candle Making Today

a significant difference to the candles burn time and still provides the gentle perfume of the wax. One cheaper beeswax alternative to emerge has been candles made from rolled foundation sheet. This is the remelted wax from beehives supplied for beekeepers to restock their hives; it comes as a yellow/brown sheet embossed with a distinctive hexagonal pattern. It is sold rolled round a wick to make a simple candle; but it does not burn well.

Stearine, first developed in the 1840s as a purified form of tallow, is still used by the candle industry and is added to candles to harden the softer paraffin wax. The average candle contains ten percent stearine, which helps increase the wax's melting point and make the candle less prone to distorting in warm weather. It is more expensive than paraffin wax but has the fashionable advantage, like beeswax, of being a renewable and sustainable raw material because it can be made from any plant or animal fat. When the rest of the world went over to paraffin wax candles at the end of the 19th century Scandinavia continued to make 100 percent stearine candles, largely because of the huge quantities of herring fish oil at their disposal. They still do so today and maintain that not only are their candles a green product, but that the quality of the light and the burn time that stearine gives is far superior to paraffin. In our more environmentally aware age manufacturers are testing the public demand for such premium green products. Stearine candles are newly popular in Germany and starting to become available in the U.K. In the same way American bayberry candles from New England are once more being made as a historic novelty. Price's are investigating the feasibility of using coconut stearine as an alternative to paraffin wax at their new plant in Sri Lanka—a curiously circular return to their roots in the 1830s, which was when they first started importing coconut oil from Sri Lanka to make their revolutionary composite candles!

But candles would never be the fashionable product they now are simply on the basis of nostalgia and quaintness. Their appeal to consumers today is just as much about modern design and lifestyle. Traditional shapes and colors are very popular, but so too are a bewildering array of new colors, scents, and designs. The challenge for candle makers has been to move beyond the simple historical associationsof candles and candle holders and produce ranges of obviously contemporary products that will complement any type of room setting. Fifty years ago the only "lifestyle" candles used in most houses were those lit in the dining room to accompany a special meal. Today there are ranges of candles for burning throughout the house: kitchen candles that

Left, Above Left, and Right: New ways of burning old candles; poured container candles can be designed to accommodate just about any setting— tinplate for the garden, ceramics for the kitchen, and frosted glass for the bathroom.

Just over a century ago candles came in white, white, or off-white; today the whole palette of color is available.

complement the smells of cooking, bathroom candles to relax in the bath with, even feng shui candles that can be used to reorient the portals of your home and protect you from the demons! One of the biggest successes for candle makers has been persuading people to use candles in the garden.

Color has remained an important part of candles but has become more fluid and changing. The huge pallette of colors now available and the speed with which new color runs can be produced has allowed candle makers to respond to the changing color schemes of the worlds of *haute couture* and interior design. Candles can now support this year's color scheme or design mood or reinforce the effect of a fragrance—a candle burning with the perfume of lavender is mauve, a chamomile one is yellow, and so on. New fashions—like the current interest in color therapy, which matches particular hues to mood changes—can be translated into candles.

Another trend is the move away from the candle holder to focus on the candle itself. A century ago the candlestick that was the object of value and an ornament to the room while the candle it contained was just the means to the light. Increasingly today that relationship is being reversed. Many of the new large candles are designed objects in their own right, not just colored but carved, sculpted, painted, appliqued, collaged, or otherwise decorated

to fit a particular design trend. The recent taste for extremely large pillar or block candles, sometimes with multiple wicks is one example of this. The scale of the candle, that relies for its effect on its sheer size and shape almost removes the need for a candle holder altogether, or reduces it to the status of residual grease pan or tray to protect the surface on which the candle stands. It is the mass, color, design, or sculptural or slab-like quality of the candle itself that now draws the eye. In a similar way the new fashion for floating candles, suspended in water, again focuses attention on the candles rather than the container—like admiring fish in a tank, rather than the detail of the aquarium that surrounds them. Another new development that similarly focuses on the candle is candle sand. This process—a pile of powdered wax into which a wick is inserted and lit—actually deconstructs the candle into a pile of loose raw material that can be shaped or assembled however one wishes.

At a time when changes in fashion accelerate and the designed life of an object becomes shorter and shorter, needing to be quickly replaced, it becomes more logical for the candle—the epitome of the ephemeral—to become the designed object in place of the candlestick. You are not left with the problem of the unfashionable candleholder left behind. This trend towards more disposable or shorter lived designs is also seen in the current popularity for poured wax lights in ornamental containers. Modeled on the night light, these container lights dispense with the notion of a separate candle and candle holder. The two are instead a single unit that is disposable, or theoretically refillable. There is no limit to the type of object that can be converted into a wax light. The container can be an obviously precious or aesthetic object—

Right: Beach pebbles and candles combine to make an elegant arrangement of contrasting forms and textures.

Right: A Chinese-style poem candle and votive light with appropriate herbal fragrances.

Candle Making Today

c o l o r e d
glass, decorated
ceramics, or chinese porcelain that
may hark back to oil burners and sim-
ple lamps or to the Victorian taste for ornamental
glass night light holders. But the principle, once
established, lends itself to all sorts of playful puns and
the witty recycling of objects not normally associated
with candles—the cup and saucer filled with a perfumed chocolate-brown wax, actual seashells or glass
fish shaped containers for lighting in the bathroom, a
terra cotta flower pot decorated with pictures of
a flower and burning a wax with that flower's fragrance, or enamel buckets for garden lights. A new
development in container lights is the gel candle—a
translucent semi-solid mineral oil produced in a
range of colors and per-
fumes in clear glass

containers—that hovers on the boundary between
candles and oil lamps

This is not to suggest that that container lights
and giant candles are about to replace the traditional
candle and candle stick altogether. What is remark-
able about the current taste for candles is the
breadth of the market and this is nowhere better
seen than in the extraordinary and imaginative
growth in candlestick and candle holder design.
Again comparisons with the same market 50 years
ago are instructive. In the 1950s, outside the rarefied
world of solid silver craftsmanship located in exclusive jewelers and the new Italian and Scandinavian
"Contemporary" designs in aluminium and stainless
steel that might be found in a few fashionable shops,
candlesticks were restricted to better class department stores who continued to stock a small variety of
reproduction brass and silver plate designs loosely
modeled on traditional Georgian and Regency styles:
a safe bet for wedding presents and dining room
ornaments.

The market for real and reproduction antique
candlesticks and lighting is still very large and clearly
continues to inform a lot of popular designs. But
today's designers are increasingly inspired by, rather
than just slavishly reproducing, the past; and they
have not been afraid to incorporate influences from
around the world as well. This post-modern melting
pot is able to mix and match a whole confection
of modernist, ethnic, repro, and ironic designs for
today's consumer. All time and space is there: a
riot of Pugin derived Gothic with black metal
medieval torch stands and ecclesiastical wrought
iron pricketts looking like instruments of medieval
torture vie with fake Stuart sconces and Georgian
candelabra. Third World tinplate lanterns from
Mexico or India are found alongside carved soapstone
and pummice stone holders from Africa, cheap

Right: This multiwicked giant pillar candle relies on its mass and
simple form for its dramatic effect.

Above: Floating candles are now a popular way to focus the attention on the candle rather than the holder.

Chinese porcelain votive lights, and earth-colored ceramics from Latin America. There are candlesticks in shiny lacquered brass, and in distressed, verdigris'd brass and in recycled green glass. Smooth modernist shapes in stainless steel and aluminium suggest the sculptures of Henry Moore while contorted clusters of steel tendrils supporting multiple sockets resemble some Art Nouveau design with added growth hormones—half plant, half candelabra.

If one were to single out just one development that has really enlarged and transformed the market for candles in Europe and the U.S. it is probably the introduction of fragrances into candles. The process is by no means a new one. The Romans sometimes used perfume in their oil lamps to disguise their odor and enhance a room; a practice that was perpetuated by wealthier Victorians, whose lamps burned *huiles parfumées* as an alternative to the rank smell of sperm lamp oil. Camphor was often added to early Christian church candles to increase the spiritual aura of the religious service and survives today in the Catholic Church's use of incense. In the 17th century musk perfume was added to the finest wax candles which were used as a kind of high status air freshener and aphrodisiac, while in New England in the 18th century it was found that the locally produced bayberry candles had a particularly fragrant odor that was most pronounced when the candle was snuffed out. It was common practice to repeatedly light and then snuff out these candles to perfume the room. The 19th century link with soap making meant that many makers who started by adding fragrances to their toilet soaps also experimented by adding it to candles as well. Price's were producing a rose perfumed candle by 1905.

What is different about perfumed candles today is the level of use. In the past they were expensive

Right: Simple but effective square candles—the harder outer layer of wax forms a container within which the flame burns down; the outer layer then functions like a translucent pane for the light to shine through.

novelties; today they are mainstream and perfume has become just as important a requirement of a candle as color. Initially these were an experiment: a novel way of perfuming a room—subtler and sexier than an aerosol spray—that combined the existing taste for candlelight with the new fashion for fragrances delivered by incense burners and oil burners. Ten years on the perfumed candle has now become a large, complex, and sophisticated market. Over half of the candles produced by the major manufacturers are now perfumed and that proportion is set to continue to increase. There are fragranced candles to complement cookery odors from the kitchen or to neutralise tobacco smoke. You can burn perfumed candles that reprise fashionable herbal and holistic treatments—Aloe Vera, St. Johns Wort, and Ericaea. Current thinking suggests that every fragrance should be purposeful and therapeutic, not merely pleasant smelling. Candle makers have looked at many other fashionable trends in fragrances and used them to inform new products. New ranges of aromachology candles—using the principles of aromatherapy—that contain small amounts of essential oils to enhance or induce a particular mood are one popular development. The current interest in Chinese herbalism has led to the introduction of a range of candles designed to suggest images of the Far East, with bamboo shaped candles, Chinese-style votive light burners, and candles decorated with ideographs, and all containing appropriate fragrances—ginseng, jasmine, or lotus blossom. New fashions, like the current interest in Dead Sea minerals and Ayurveda, an ancient Indian science that matches fragrances with energy centers in the body, are likely to inform future ranges of perfumed candles.

If we turn from the candle shops to look at some of the manufacturers we can see how these have

Right: Playing games with bees; hive and bee-shaped candles and containers decorated with bee motifs, all burning with the fragrance of wax and honey.

Candle Making Today

Candle Making Today

Candle Making Today

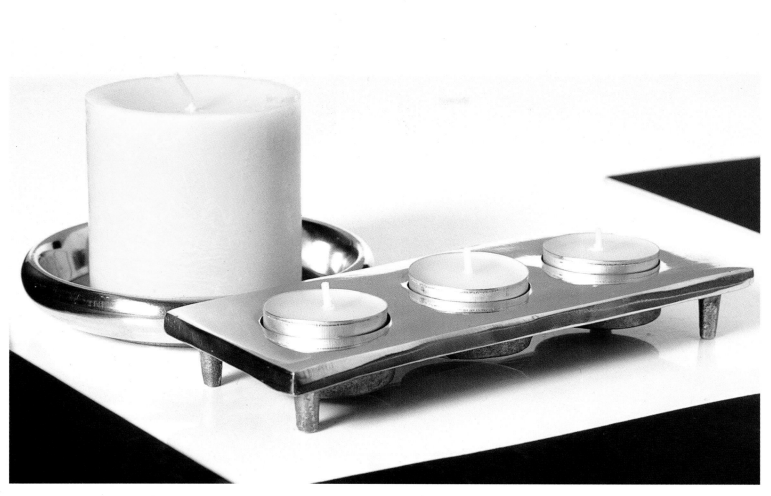

Above: Simple designs and smooth lines in aluminum work well with uncolored night lights and candles.

been affected by the extraordinary recent growth in the industry. At one end of the spectrum is an international manufacturer, Price's Patent Candle Company, now the largest and oldest candle maker in the U.K. At the other end are a host of much smaller candle makers, barely one step up from cottage industry.

Prices have two modern high volume plants, one in Oxfordshire and one in Sri Lanka turning out 3,500 tons of wax candle and other products a year. The candle market nationally is growing at about ten percent a year, but Price's has seen its turnover increase seven-fold in ten years. Candle molding machines, the 19th century's contribution to mass

Left: Eastern influences; these glass hanging night light holders deliberately evoke the form and the effect of Chinese paper lanterns.

production in the industry, are still used; but this elderly technology now only comprises about a tenth of their production. The molding machines now used have over 2,000 molds on a circular frame; they are force cooled using chilled water to push production to 500 candles every 25 minutes. They are used to produce traditional solid color and overdipped candles for dinner tables and for the catering trade.

Various cold processes using powdered wax are now the main source of volume candle production. Half of Price's candle output is now produced by using extrusion or compression processes. The extrusion process uses powdered paraffin wax, which is forced through a small orifice where it consolidates round a wick, producing a continuous length of candle, that is then cut to length. When first developed it could only be used for the cheapest and most utilitar-

Candle Making Today

ian of candles, like household and birthday cake candles. There were limits to the diameter and quality of finish that could be achieved and the extruded candles were all straight sided. Extrusion nowadays is considerably more sophisticated and is used to produce various types of tapered candles, shaved to shape, either overdipped with other colors or made with solid color wax; perfume can even be added to these candles. The other cold process now used is compression; it works on the same cold pressure principle but for individual units rather than a continuous length of candle. All night lights and tea lights are produced by this method.

The newest process introduced at Price's is for their range of poured candles, which now amounts to about a third of their output. This is a new candle product that has quickly grown from nothing and reflects the current popularity of colored and perfumed wax lights in elegant or unusual containers—colored glass, ceramics, sea shells, novelty tins, or whatever. Pouring molten wax into the wicked container is an ancient process harking back to night light manufacture and the earliest molded candles, but in its new incarnation it is a reflection of the way that candle design and use has changed so dramatically over the last ten years.

What is interesting about the candle market today is the way it is allowing smaller manufacturers to re-emerge. If the pattern in the 19th century was one of a growing industrial scale of production and the creation of larger and larger companies who bought out the smaller firms, then by contrast the end of the 20th century has seen the reappearance of small manufacturers with distinctive products. These small craft ventures can be traced back to the growing interest in folk traditions and cottage industries that developed in the 1960s. Candle making was one of many lost skills to be disinterred, demystified, and made accessible then through a host of "How To Do It" books and do-it-yourself kits. For the first time since the days of the rushlight, it became practicable to make your own candles in the home.

What started as a novel hobby was in retrospect the entry point for a whole new tier of smaller craft candle

Left and Right: Brass was one of the earliest metals to be used for candlestick manufacture, and these modern sticks hark back to an earlier Gothic taste in a variety of metals.

Above: Chinese style "bamboo" pillar candles, appropriately fragranced with jasmine, ginseng, and lotus blossom.

Left: Simple candlestick designs that would once have been turned in wood are today recast in recycled frosted glass.

Right: Art Nouveau style revived for this delicate night light holder in glass and black metal.

makers. What the new do-it-yourself candle makers could achieve that the big manufacturers couldn't was a range of color, technique, and shape that hand crafting or small scale production runs could bring. By the late 1960s and 1970s the candle had become something of a counter-cultural icon. It was one of the necessary accoutrements for the post-Woodstock generation along with joss-sticks, black ceilings, and the right sort of music on the turntable. People need-ed candles to match their mood, and plain white household candles just didn't hit the spot. When Price's had first started selling unrefined palm oil candles in the 1840s no one would buy them because

they were orange; now there was a whole new market for bright orange, brown, and black candles and no one was making them any more!

Many of the new candle makers making distinctive products today have emerged from the hobbyist tradition. These people have graduated from melting paraffin wax in old saucepans over the gas cooker and using homemade candle molds with bits of string for wicks. What perhaps started as a way of making candles for their own use and gifts for friends then turned into a small sideline to supplement a student grant or to earn money at weekends. Selling from stalls in street markets, at craft fairs, and music festivals, these products of the counter culture started to edge into the mainstream. The new candle makers moved out of the kitchen and into the garden shed, bought themselves some bigger equipment—gas burners and bains maries replaced the

Above: Candles enhance even the simplest activity; family cards played by candlelight during the 1977 New York electricity black out.

Right: Perfumed candles to complement food; hot chocolate and Earl Grey tea are appropriate fragrances for the breakfast table.

two jam pans on the kitchen stove—and started going into production.

Suddenly by the 1990s there was a genuine market to supply. Everyone was suddenly burning candles again and the new specialist candle shops with their huge ranges of designed and perfumed products showed both the enormous size of the market and the demand for unique or quirky products. But how could they compete? What could they do that the big manufacturers couldn't immediately do better and cheaper?

The new firm of E & S Churchill are a good example of this process. A brother and sister partnership

Candle Making Today

Candle Making Today

Above Left, Left, Above, and Right: Price's state of the art candle plants now produce over 3,500 tons of candle products a year. Here we see wax mixing and continuous production machinery for the manufacture of night lights and container candles in the factory at Bicester, Oxfordshire.

Candle Making Today

who have been making candles commercially for the last three years, they emerged via the kitchen stove and garden shed route and now occupy commercial workshop space. They employ four staff and have a production turnover of just 1,300 candles a week. Their candles are found at the more fashionable London street markets, by mail order, and through a few high class retailers.

Apart from being a very small scale operation, what distinguishes their products from the main-stream is their commitment to high quality materials and handcrafting. The business idea grew out of their own dissatisfaction with the aesthetics and burning quality of many commercially available candles and was further driven by a commitment to using natural products wherever possible. They produce a range of traditional beeswax pillar candles and it is the quality and high percentage beeswax of the candles that are the strengths of their product. While factory "beeswax church candles" for the domestic market

Above: Beeswax candles at Churchill's workshop; wicked and freshly poured in their glass molds they resemble nothing so much as tall jars of liquid honey.

Right: Counter culture candles; a peripatetic candle seller with bicycle outside The Candles Shop in Bond Street Fashion Market, London, in the early 1970s. This was one of the first dedicated candle shops to open in England.

only contain ten percent beeswax and even real church candles have between 20 and 25 percent, Churchill's candles contain 30 percent. Their product recalls the historical arguments of previous centuries about the superiority of beeswax over tallow. Churchill's beeswax candles burn more brightly, more slowly, and smell pleasanter than their paraffin wax rivals. Their largest pillar candle has a burn time of over 1,000 hours. In the age of the multicolored and fragranced candle they refuse to add any color or perfume to their products and rely on the natural color and fragrance of the wax. They also refuse to bleach their candles, arguing that the yellow-brown tone is the natural color of the wax.

Candle Making Today

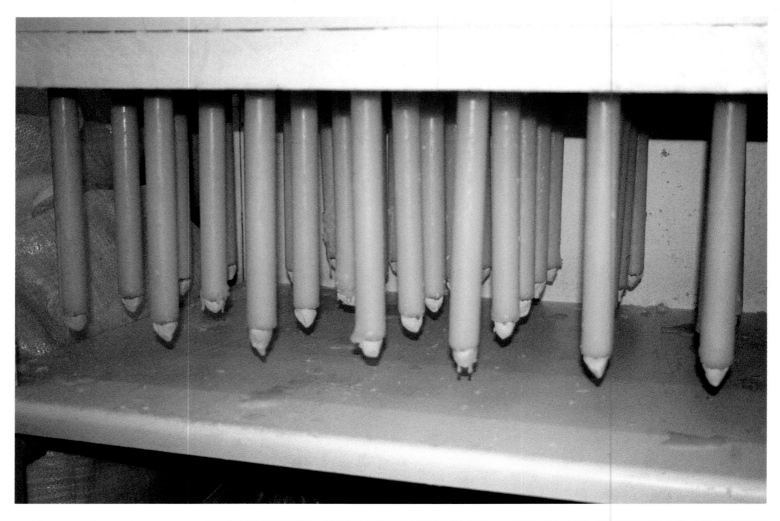

Above: Candle manufacture at Churchill's workshop; rows of hand poured molded candles cooling.

Right: Candle manufacture at Churchill's workshop; the cooled beeswax candles are ready to be gently pulled from their glass molds.

Candle Making Today

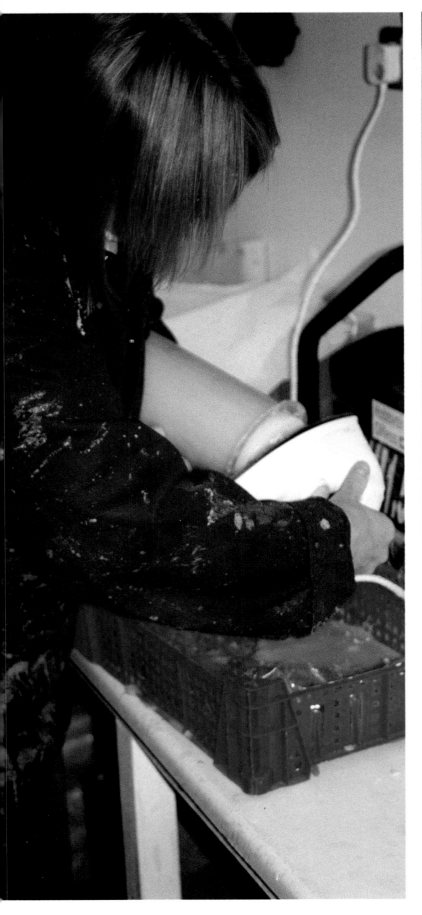

Left and Above: Candle manufacture at Churchill's workshop; gently sliding the glass mold from off a cooled beeswax candle and then smoothing off the base with an electric iron.

Candle Making Today

This is an interesting take on the old arguments about candle color. A hundred and fifty years of paraffin wax has completely destroyed the old association of whiteness with quality. Today consumers assume that yellow-brown, off-white, or ivory candles, whether in paraffin or beeswax, are somehow more historically authentic because all cheap household candles are white.

Their workshop space is an interesting throwback with echoes of the preindustrial candle workshop of the 18th century. Drawn glass molds with hand threaded, plaited wicks supplied by a traditional ropemaker, stand in rows along the benches. The electric pump for pouring the wax is the one concession to the post-industrial age, but the candle maker still has to carefully fill each mold in turn, returning to top it up when it has cooled. Using glass means that Churchill's are able to mold their high percentage beeswax candles; if they used metal molds they would stick and not extract smoothly. They are even considering producing a 90 percent beeswax candle if there is sufficient demand. The cooled candles are extracted by hand, have their bases smoothed by a hot iron, their wicks trimmed, and are ready for sale.

If Churchill's found its niche market by a rediscovery of hand processes and its use of natural, pure materials that would appeal to more environmentally aware consumers who were prepared to pay a premium for greener products, then the candlemaker Gary Stewart from Oxfordshire has taken a different but equally distinctive route. Another outgrown do-it-yourself hobbyist, his main job now is beekeeping. Interestingly he refuses to use his bees' wax for candle manufacture. He regards it as too valuable. You can either farm bees for the wax or for the honey; and as Gary's principal business is brewing mead from the honey, the wax gets returned to the hives to allow the bees to concentrate on honey production.

Left: Candle manufacture at Churchill's workshop; pouring the beeswax/paraffin wax mixture and then removing the wick holders after cooling.

Gary's candles are made from paraffin wax. Like the candle makers of the 18th century before him who made their candles in the winter and then worked on their farms in the summer, Gary's work is seasonal. His candles are only made during the six months the bees are dormant.

The candles are all hand molded using standard mold shapes. What distinguishes his products from the factory ones is the imaginitive use of color and hand finishing to create unique and startling designs. The dipped and carved candles start with a solid color candle, which is overdipped in two or more contrasting colors and then "carved" using a hot iron to part-reveal the layers of color beneath. Another dramatic technique is the use of solid lump wax and powder dye in candles to create dramatic and unique colored candles. Solid lumps of white wax and powder dye are added to a part filled mold; the solid lumps set randomly in the cooling wax while the color from the powder dye seeps slowly down through the rest of the candle to make intriguing swirls of color. Perfume is not added to the candles; instead Gary suggests carefully adding a drop of essential oil to the molten wax at the top of an already lit candle. This allows you to vary the fragrance according to your mood.

Gary Stewart making candles in his workshop.
Left, overdipping solid color candles with a contrasting color;
Above Right, "carving" overdipped black candles with an electric iron to reveal the brighter colors beneath; **Right**, the variety of effects that can be obtained from heat "carving" with an electric iron.

Candle Making Today

Candle Making Today

5 Making Your Own Candles

Five hundred years ago nearly every candle was homemade. One of the compelling points was simplicity of manufacture; dip candles and rush lights made by immersing linen or rush wicks in a tub of molten fat used a low-level technology that was accessible to even the poorest household. These simple tallow candles were still being made in some remote rural areas in England and Wales at the beginning of the 20th century, and one could, if one chose, faithfully recreate those processes today, complete with the smoke, the smells, and all their other technical limitations. However most do-it-yourself candle take on board the scientific improvements of the last couple of centuries. If you are going to make your own candles you might as well use paraffin wax, candle molds, and a braided wick that will not need snuffing. Gathering rushes from the riverbank and slaughtering your own cows and sheep to extract the dense fat located around the kidneys is strictly for the historical enthusiast.

Just as candles have grown in popularity over the last three decades, so too the craft of home candle making has been rediscovered and popularized. Starter kits are now found in toy shops and art shops containing enough of the basic equipment and small quantities of the raw materials to get the beginner started. Specialist candle craft shops have also appeared to supply the serious amateur with the full range of waxes, wicks, molds, and other equipment while many of the larger manufacturers of waxes and wicks are now also prepared to supply on a retail basis to the hobbyist. There is an immense published literature on the subject to which this chapter adds no more than a simple summary.

Materials and Equipment

If you buy a candle making kit you will be supplied with all you need. If you are starting from scratch you will need:

- Thermometer (kitchen variety with a range beyond boiling, i.e 212°F or100°C)
- Double boiler (reduces the risk of burning or overheating the wax, but you can use an old saucepan with a thick base)
  - Dipping cans (for producing dip candles and for overdipping mold candles)
- Candle molds
- Wicking needle and mold sealant (for use with candle molds)
- Measuring jug, bowls, and scales
- Heat source
- Wax (paraffin wax and stearine are essential for mold candles; microcrystalline wax and beeswax may both also be needed)
- Wicks
- Color dyes (available as powder or disc)
- Perfume (check that it is oil soluble and not spirit based)

Above: The home candle makers
equipment assembled and ready
to go. From the left there is a
pouring jug, spools of wick and
some mold sealant, packs of
precolored paraffin wax granules,
natural paraffin wax with
thermometer and measuring scoop,
a smaller quantity of stearine and
a selection of molds in clear plastic
and metal. To the right the spatula
and dyes in stick and disk form are
resting on some sheets of beeswax.

Making Your Own Candles

Basic Safety

Always keep the wax temperature below 100°C; if you use a double water boiler you will never be able to exceed this. If you are using a single saucepan always use a thermometer. Wax smokes and gives off toxic fumes above 100°C. Never heat wax above 177°C or you will approach the flash point at which it will spontaneously combust. Avoid using a naked flame as your heat source. Never use water on wax fires—a damp cloth, pan lid, or fire blanket should be used to smother the flames. Don't tip molten wax down a sink or drain; you will probably block it. Wear sensible clothes and work in an adequate work space. Be extremely careful when handling molten wax; you can use rubber gloves to prevent scalding; in extremis wax can remove your fingerprints for several weeks. Small children and inquisitive pets are best kept in a separate room.

How to Begin

You will need a controlled heat source that can maintain wax at a constant temperature during manufacture. Electricity is preferred to gas because there is no naked flame. If you use a bain marie or double boiler system this will ensure the wax temperature stays below 100°C. If you are using a single container for melting wax you have to be careful that the wax does not burn on the base of the container or get too hot; a thermometer becomes essential. The inner container for the wax must be of iron, steel, or aluminium—definitely not copper or brass; if you are adding beeswax to your candles then iron too should be avoided.

Left: A selection of primed and unprimed wicks and dye sticks and disks.

Below: A selection of different candle molds: on the right is a two piece globe mold, in the foreground shaped flexible molds.

Above: Using a bain marie or double boiler to gently melt the paraffin wax, the wick is then primed by giving it a thin coating of wax.

Above: Candle molds with primed wicks held taut in place with a blob of mold sealant at the bottom and stick across the top of the mold.

Most candle makers use paraffin wax on the grounds of convenience, availability, and cost. Beeswax is extremely expensive, but can be added in quite small proportions to considerable effect—ten percent or even five percent added to paraffin wax will significantly improve the burn time, hardness, color, and perfume of the candle. Most do-it-yourself chandlers will also want to add small amounts of more expensive stearine and microcrystalline wax, especially to mold candles.

Anyone reading the earlier chapters on the history of candle manufacture and the development of the snuffless wick will have already realized how important this seemingly trivial component actually is. If you just use a bit of string for a wick, then your candle will almost certainly smoke, gutter, or otherwise burn badly. It pays to purchase proper plaited and braided wicks. Select your wick according to your candle size. The larger diameter your intended candle, the thicker a wick you require. If the wick is too thick, the flame is too large and causes the wax to run down the sides and the candle to melt away; if too thin then the flame is insufficient to melt the pool of wax at the top of the candle and the flame burns itself down in a small hole at the centre of the candle until extinguished through lack of oxygen. Wick suppliers will provide a conversion guide that identifies appropriate wick thickness for candle diameter.

Different Techniques

You will need to make a decision on what candle making technique to use. The basic processes that were used by the 18th century chandler of pouring,

Above: Adding color to the wax; a piece of solid dye is added to the already melted natural paraffin wax and then gently dissolved.

dipping, or molding can all still be used in the home but some are more practical than others. You can make candles by pouring; the technique is still used today for very tall church candles and can in theory be carried out in the home. It requires a lot of room, but no very special equipment. A wick or wicks are suspended above the container of molten wax and a ladle is used to pour the wax down the length of the wick; the excess falls back into the wax container. It is a highly skilled craft and not a very sensible entry point for the beginner so we shall not go into detail about the process here. Dipping is still the simplest method of manufacture and is a good way of starting candle making. It is also the home process that can most easily be adopted for producing reasonable quantities of candles. Molding is a slower process that works well for one-off decorative candles in unusual shapes or of a large diameter.

Dip Candles

Using just a single length of wick and a dipping can you can make a pair of hand-dipped candles as a first project. Double-over the length of wick and weight the two ends. Take two pounds of plain paraffin wax and gently heat in the boiler to 71°C. Pour the molten wax into the dipping can; this needs to be deeper than the length of the wick with space at the top to allow for the displacement caused by the dipping; if you are using a ten inch wick then you will need a 12 inch can. Hold the top of the loop and dip both wicks in the can, leaving for three minutes; remove the wicks, pull them straight and allow to cool. This longer first dipping is to prime the wicks and allows all the air and moisture to escape. Subsequent dippings of the wick need only remain in the wax for about six seconds and then should be smoothly withdrawn to avoid surface irregularities building up.

Far Left: Pouring the molds; the candle on the right has already cooled. The molten wax is poured smoothly into the wicked mold, making sure not to overfill.

Left and Below: The cooled candles are extracted by gently pulling them from the mold using the protruding end of the wick at the base.

Between dippings the candles can be hung to cool in the air or plunged into a bowl of water; make sure the two candles do not touch each other while this takes place. Repeat the process until the pair of candles are built up to the required thickness. Cut off the weights, cut or melt the candle bases smooth, trim the wick, and your first pair of dip candles are complete.

The natural taper of a hand dipped candle is extremely attractive. If you want to produce these in quantity then you will need to move on from the rather laborious process of dipping a single pair of wicks. If you use a larger diameter dipping can or trough and suspend a series of wicks along a stick or around a wheel you can produce large numbers of candles at a go.

Mold Candles

Moulding candles is now the most popular method of manufacture for homemade candles. It is the

Above: Even simpler to make and using no heat are these "candle sand" candles. A suitable container is filled with the paraffin wax granules and a primed wick is inserted into it.

Right: Chinese poem candle and ceramic pot candle.

availability through candle craft shops of an enormous choice of molds in a variety of shapes and sizes that has contributed to the upsurge in do-it-yourself candle making over the last 30 years. Molding is considerably slower than dipping and requires a greater initial outlay on equipment. But its advantages are the production of larger and more decorative candles where shape, color, or surface texture are more important than its utility.

The technique is simple; the hollow mold has a wick suspended through it, is filled with wax and, when cool, the candle is removed. In addition to wax and wick the basic equipment for making these candles are candle mold(s), a wicking needle and some mold sealant. Molds can be rigid or flexible and made from metal, plastic, glass, rubber, or PVC. There is a tremendous choice of shape and size in the market. It

❀ 143 ❀

Making Your Own Candles

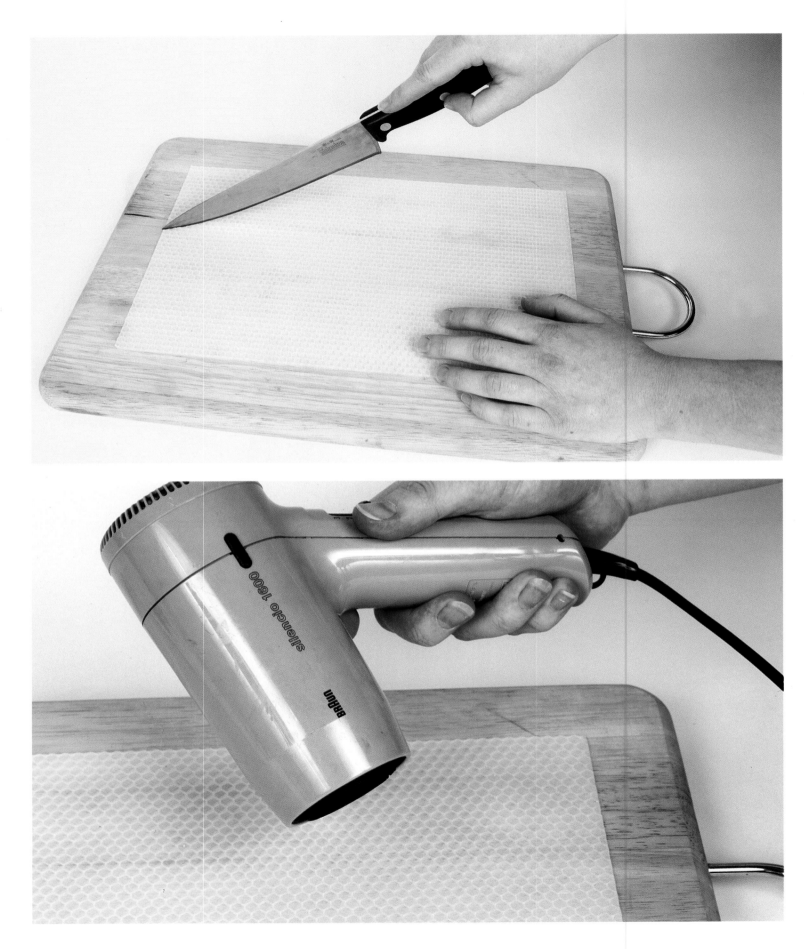

Making Your Own Candles

Simple rolled sheet wax candles—
for the hobbyist who doesn't want to
get burned fingers.

Left and Above Left: The sheet is
cut to size and softened using gentle
heat.

Right and Above Right: A wick is
inserted and the wax rolled tightly
around it.

Overleaf: Simple floating candles
can be made from biscuit or cookie
cutters, sweet, or petit-four molds,
or even tart tins.

Making Your Own Candles

is probably best to start with a rigid mold; the flexible rubber and PVC ones come in more interesting textured shapes, but have a tendency to perish with prolonged use if stearine is used in the mix.

The mold has to be wicked up with a primed wick (as described in the process for dip candles). This is threaded through the wick hole in the base of the mold and secured centrally at the top by attaching it to the wicking needle or a small stick across the lip of the mold. The wick is then pulled tight through the wick hole and secured by a lump of mold sealant; this serves the double purpose of holding the wick taut and sealing the base of the mold—you can check the latter by putting the mold in a bowl of water.

For dip candles it is possible to use pure paraffin wax. When making mold candles it is necessary to use a harder wax so that the candle can be extracted from the mold without sticking. To achieve this we use a higher melting point paraffin wax (60°-68°C) and add stearine (ten percent) to improve the shrinkage of the cooled candle. Microcrystalline wax (one percent) can also be added to this mixture to further increase the hardness and give a good surface finish to the candle. If you are making a single mold candle and want to calculate the amount of wax required, fill the mould to the top with water and pour this out into a measuring jug. For each fluid ounce of water use an ounce of wax (100ml equals 90g). Heat this mixture of waxes to 85°C and transfer to a pouring vessel with a spout. Pour slowly and fill the mold to just below the top. Be careful not to overfill. Tap the mold to encourage any trapped air bubbles to rise to the surface. It then needs to be left to part-cool. As the candle cools the wax shrinks and contracts away from the wall of the mold and also around the base of the wick where a shallow well or depression forms. This has to be topped up after an hour; break the surface skin of the wax around the wick and fill with more wax at the original pouring temperature. It is essential when topping up that you do not add wax above the original height of the candle or this will get between the walls of the mold and the cooling candle and make extraction difficult.

The cooling process can be accelerated by using a water bath; the weighted mold is stood upright in a larger bowl with cool water that comes up the full height of the wax in the mold. However, if the water is too cold—below 10°C—it will actually damage the surface of the candle. When the candle has fully cooled it can be gently pulled from the mold by the knotted wick at the base. If you are using a rubber mold this is simply peeled back and off. Cut out this knotted wick from the base using a sharp knife and trim the top wick to an appropriate length. With very large diameter candles you may want to smooth the base flat using a heat source like an old electric iron.

Color, Texture, and Fragrance

The basic requirements for making dip and mold candles have been described using plain white paraffin wax. However most do-it-yourself candle makers are driven by the desire to produce unique and decorative candles for their home or as personalized gifts. And this may involve the use of color, perfume, carving, sculpting, and other techniques.

Color is readily available in the form of powder or disk dyes. Color dye needs to be used sparingly and don't be tempted to exceed the manufacturers recommended ratios. A very darkly colored candle may look impressive but it provides a poor source of illumination; the dark color of the wax absorbs much more of the light. Color dyes are best added to the molten stearine and carefully mixed in before being added in turn to the molten paraffin wax.

Right: Ceramic container candles.

Making Your Own Candles

Making Your Own Candles

Candle chic in the bath; a selection of fragranced and sand candles to make your bath even more relaxing.

Making Your Own Candles

or you can experiment with part filling larger molds and containers. Another approach is to produce shallow discs of wax by pouring small quantities onto grease proof paper. These can be added to in sections, peeled of and assembled round a central wick to produce floating flower petal candles. These candles also rely for their effect on the aesthetics of the larger water container; so get your finest glass dish, fill it to the brim to keep the flames away from glass edges.

Candles for Children

Most parents rightly shudder at the thought of their precious offspring fiddling with double boilers and molten paraffin wax. Fortunately there are some safe methods of candle manufacture that do not involve any heat and can allow your children to participate in your hobby and make their own simple designs. Candle sand is one safe and simple option that involves putting a wick into a pile of powdered paraffin wax and lighting it.

Slightly more creative than candle sand are candles made from rolling up sheet wax. The simplest to get hold of is actually beeswax foundation sheet. This was originally produced for bee keepers to restock their hives with wax, and it comes preembossed with the hexagonal design of the wax comb. It is now available through candle supplies shops as well. To make a rolled candle from foundation sheet simply cut a rectangle of sheet for a parallel sided candle, or a triangle for a tapered candle. Cut an appropriate length of wick and tightly roll the sheet around the wick core, taking care to keep a flat base. This is best done in a warm room so the wax is easy to handle; to finish the candle off you simply push the final edge of the sheet into the candle. The projecting wick will need a little wax rubbed onto it to make it flammable. These are extremely simple and safe to make, will actually burn and have all the perfume of an expensive beeswax candle.

Even more fun for younger children, if you can get hold of it, is the really soft modeling wax than can be kneaded and shaped by hand, cut using biscuit cutters and rolled up with a wick inside. Tactile, safe, versatile, and fun the end result will actually burn just like a real candle.

Exotica

Once you have molded, colored, and perfumed your candle, you may be content just to light it and admire it. But for many people, the process doesn't stop there as there are a whole range of techniques of surface decoration that can be employed to further enhance the candle.

Dried leaves, petals, flowers, and grasses can be easily appliquéd to the side of a candle. These can be pressed into place using a warm knife. Ensure that the items you are attaching are completely dried through. When you are happy with the design, encapsulate it by giving the finished candle a final overdip in hot clear wax.

The appliqué principle can be applied to many other objects—small sea shells, fragments of colored glass or mosaic tile, beads and sequins, small coins, or even chunks of brightly colored wax—you can make your own list. This technique works best with a larger diameter pillar candle using a slightly smaller wick so that the decorated outer wall of the candle doesn't burn down, but is instead illuminated from within by the candle flame. It also works to greatest effect on a white or pale colored candle against which the darker appliquéd surface objects show up like stained glass.

Similarly dramatic effects can be obtained by painting the surface of the candle. You can use acrylic paints—although you may have problems with the candle burning evenly if you use too much. A more effective technique is to paint with molten paraffin wax. Make up very small amounts of deeply

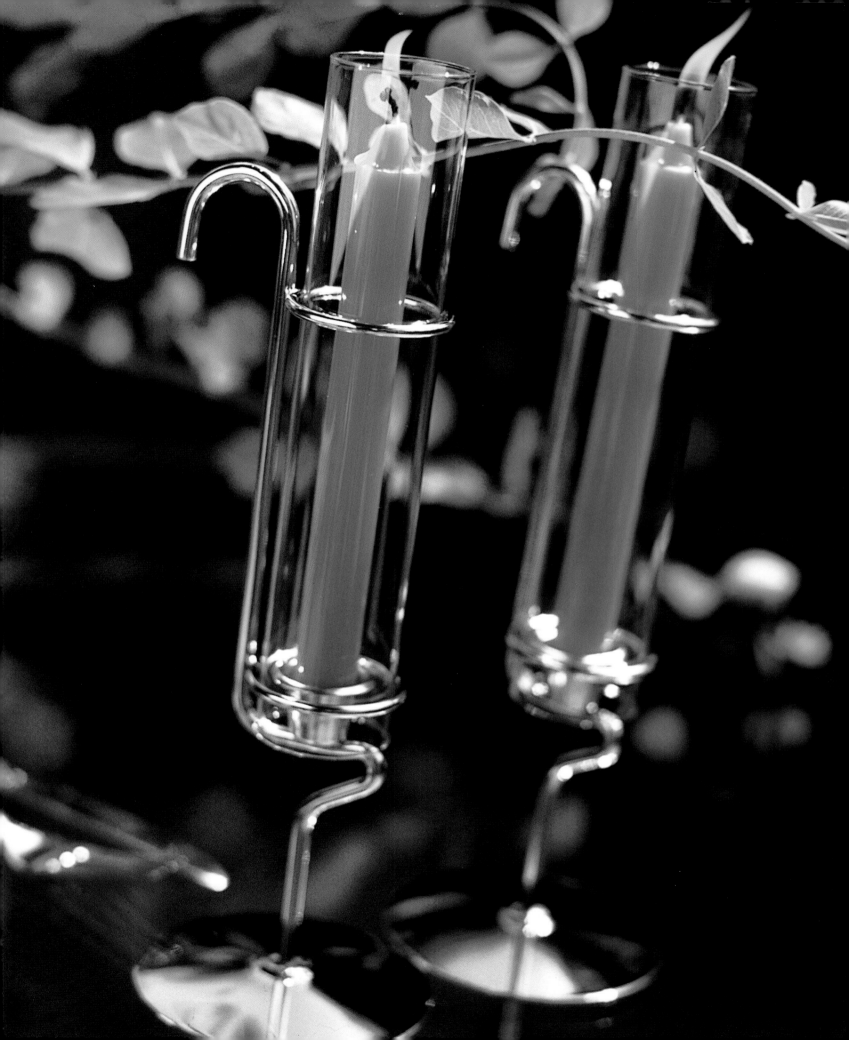

dyed wax in an old egg poacher and apply with an old paintbrush. Remember to keep the brush soft by leaving it in the molten wax. You have to get it right first time as you cannot remove the colored wax once it has been applied.

There are other dramatic surface effects that are actually done at the molding stage. Extraordinary pierced and perforated candles can be used by adding crushed ice to the candle mold before the wax is poured in. The ice creates pockets of water within the cooling candle that run off when it is removed from the mold. This works best if you actually insert a narrow diameter candle into the center of t he mold and pack the ice around it; if you use a bare wick the melting ice will affect the candle's burning qualities. Chunk candles use the same principle as ice candles, only here chunks of different darker colored wax are added to the mold and the effect is not to create voids and spaces but instead areas of bright or contrasting color deep within the body of the candle. Chunk candles are a good way of recycling left over wax from previous candle projects.

Sand Candles

One delightfully simple candle that doesn't require any expensive equipment to make can be produced by molding in damp sand. It has the added advantage that each candle can be a complete one-off, shaped to whatever design you wish. The principle is that used in metal casting. The mold shape is formed in a box or bucket of damp sand. You can either dig out a random shape or bury an object that you want to copy. The molten wax is slowly poured into the hole. When part cooled, a hole for the wick is pushed through the center using a knitting needle. After the primed wick has been inserted it is sealed in place with a little more molten wax. When fully cooled the candle can be dug out of its sand pit. The sand adheres to the surface of the candle, which in itself gives it an interesting color and granular texture, which you can deliberately contrast with the wax color. If you like the sand effect, increasing the temperature of the wax will cause more to adhere; if you use a low melting point wax you can cast candles from which the sand will easily brush off.

If you like the freedom of design that sand candles gives, then you might also want to experiment with producing your own molds from other materials or from cast-off packaging. One-shot molds can be created from old glass bottles and containers; you just have to be careful breaking the mold to get the candle out. Discarded plastic packaging, suitably drilled to accommodate a wick, offers plenty of opportunities—and I understand that some people actually quite like their candles closely resembling a yoghurt pot. Another really popular candle can be produced by cutting your child's plastic football in half. Heavily textured paper and wrappings can create interesting effects; corrugated cardboard, heavily embossed wallpaper, scrunched up greaseproof paper or aluminium foil—they can all improvize as temporary molds sufficient for cooling the hot wax of your own imagination.

Right: Tin plate candle lantern burning night lights.

Making Your Own Candles

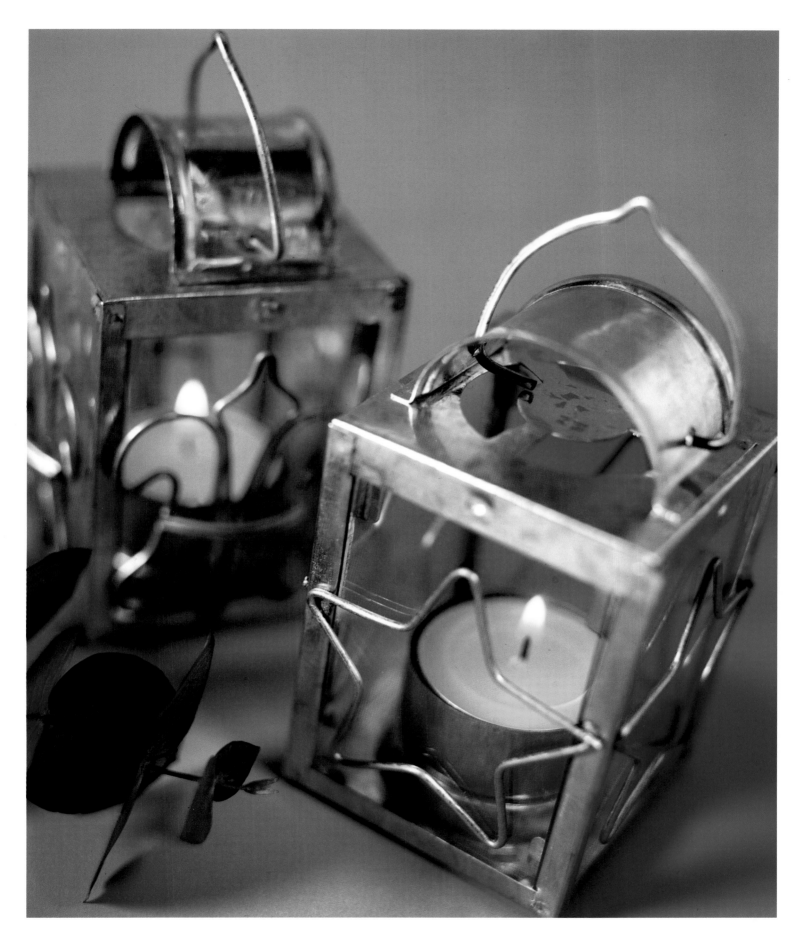

Making Your Own Candles

Index

Index